SERVSAFE FOOD MANAGER CERTIFICATION STUDY GUIDE 2024:

NOTES AND OVER 240 REVIEW QUESTIONS FOR THE SERVSAFE FOOD MANAGER EXAM

In addition, a part of the information included in this the book has been obtained through the use of ServSafe Manager Book (7th ED Revised, English), and other reliable resources and agencies that play a role in keeping food safe.

Table of Contents

Food Safety Manager Certification Study Guide 2024

Food Safety Manager Certification Review Questions

SECTION 1:
The Basics

Food Safety Manager Study Guide Section 1 | The Basics

Government Agencies that Play a Role in Keeping Food Safe

There are several government agencies that play a role in keeping food safe. The three (3) key players that we discuss in this study guide are:

1. FDA
2. USDA
3. CDC

U.S. Food & Drug Administration (FDA)
What does the FDA do?
- Scientific Research
- Issues the food code which is used by local agencies to regulate food service
  - The Food Code includes recommended practices/procedures, **but it is not a set of laws**
  - FDA **cannot require** states to adopt the Food Code
- Inspects food that crosses state lines
- Provides training and technical support

U.S. Department of Agriculture (USDA)
What does the USDA do?
- Makes sure meat, poultry, and eggs are safely packaged and correctly labeled
- Inspects food processing plants
- Inspects food shipped to suppliers

Centers for Disease Control (CDC)
What does the CDC do?
- Handles cases of diseases and outbreaks

Foodborne Illness vs. Outbreak

Foodborne illness- any illness resulting from eating contaminated food.

Outbreak- two (2) or more cases of people getting sick from eating contaminated food.
- The State and Local Regulatory Authority will investigate the claim; and a lab will confirm the outbreak.
- Affected persons will typically have the same symptoms.

Any time a foodborne illness linked to an establishment occurs, there is a high probability that an outbreak could occur as well.

Five (5) Most Common Risk Factors for Foodborne Illness

As identified by the CDC, the five (5) most common risk factors for foodborne illness are:
1. Purchasing food from unsafe sources
2. Failing to cook food correctly
3. Holding food at incorrect/improper temperatures
4. Using contaminated equipment
5. Poor personal hygiene

Test Tip: Handwashing is the best way to prevent a virus or foodborne illness.
- Must be done properly
- Must follow all steps (*outlined in Section 2*)

Four Types of Contamination

There are four (4) types of contamination that serve as threats to food safety. These different types of contamination are:

1. Biological Contamination
2. Chemical Contamination
3. Physical Contamination
4. Intentional/Deliberate Contamination

Note: Contamination may be accidental or intentional/deliberate.

Biological Contamination
- Bacteria, viruses, parasites, toxins, pathogens
- May naturally occur in some plants, mushrooms, and seafood
- Cooking or freezing **does not** destroy toxins

Chemical Contamination
- Ex: Bleach, ammonia, detergent, and other cleaning solutions
- Chemicals should:
  - Be stored on the bottom shelf/away from food
  - Have a clear and legible label with a common name if not in its original container (Ex: Plastic spray bottle labeled Clorox/Bleach)
  - Have a Safety Data Sheet (SDS) on file
    - Informs staff of safe use and hazards of chemicals used in the operation
- All staff should be trained on how to properly use chemicals

Physical Contamination
- Examples:
    - Hair and hair accessories
    - False nails, nail polish, and false eyelashes
    - Plastic Wrap
    - Band-Aids/Bandages
    - Bones and Eggshells

Intentional/Deliberate Contamination

Intentional/Deliberate Contamination may come from terrorists, unhappy staff, competitors, and anyone that wants to tamper with the food in the establishment.

The **FDA issued the A.L.E.R.T. initiative/acronym** to help restaurant employees prevent intentional/deliberate contamination. **A.L.E.R.T.** stands for:

Assure
Look
Employees
Reports
Threat

Assure
- Buy from approved and reputable suppliers only

Look
- Look at/inspect all packages received immediately

Employees
- Know who should be in the kitchen

Reports
- Keep accurate reports of daily activities and report suspicious activity

Threat
- Know who to contact when there is a threat to food safety

Time and Temperature Control

Controlling temperature is important in order to prevent time-temperature abuse.

Time-temperature abuse occurs when:
- Food is **_not being held_** at the right temperature for the right amount of time

- Food is ***not being cooked*** to the right temperature for the right amount of time
- Food is ***not being reheated*** to the right temperature for the right amount of time

Holding Temperatures for Foods

Cold foods should be kept on ice, refrigerated or frozen to a **maximum** temperature of **41°F**. (no higher)

> Ex: Dairy products should be kept in the refrigerator at a temperature of no more than **41°F**.

Clarification: Would you want to eat yogurt that is 90°F? No, because no one wants to eat hot yogurt.

Hot foods should be kept at a minimum temperature of **135°F**. (no lower)

> Ex: Lasagna on a hot buffet should be kept/held for service at a temperature of **135°F** or more.

Clarification: Would you want to eat lasagna that is 48°F? No, because no one wants to eat cold lasagna.

Temperature Danger Zone (TDZ)

This zone is **41°F to 135°F**. The **TDZ** is the area in which bacteria and pathogens grow and flourish.

Food left in the TDZ for ***more than four (4) hours*** should be **thrown away**.

Extreme Danger Zone:

This zone is **70°F to 125°F**. The extreme danger zone is the range that promotes a **rapid growth** of bacteria and pathogens.

Temperature/Time Controlled for Safety (TCS)

Use the acronym **FAT TOM** to remember Temperature/Time Controlled for Safety.

Remembering **FAT TOM** will help you to identify the factors associated with the growth of bacteria if temperature and/or time are not properly regulated.

Food (Bacteria grows well in foods like carbs and proteins)
Acidity (Bacteria grows well in 4.6 pH to 7.0 pH range | neutral to slightly acidic)
Temperature (Bacteria grows well in the the TDZ range of **41°F to 135°F**)
Time (Food should not be in the TDZ for more than 4 hours)
Oxygen (Bacteria requires oxygen to grow)
Moisture (Bacteria grows well when there is high water activity)

Common TCS Foods include:

- Chopped leafy greens
- Cut melons (**Exception to note**: May be held at **70°F** for up to four (4) hours as long as the initial temperature was not higher than **70°F**)
- Cut tomatoes
- Soy based products
- Sprouts
- Olive oil (and other oils) infused with garlic/herbs (not plain oils)

Test Tip: Some foods only become **TCS** foods once they are **cut**.
Ex: A whole watermelon is not a TCS food, **but a watermelon slice is a TCS food.**

More About Sprouts

- TCS food that is commonly used in multiple cuisines (Sprouts are used in many Thai and Vietnamese dishes.)
- Grown with water
- A prime breeding zone for bacteria because of how they are grown

Examples of TCS Proteins include:

- Pork chops
- Red meat
- Poultry and Lamb
- Fish
- Raw Shrimp and other shellfish or crustaceans
- Intact and Messed with Meat

Intact Meat vs. Messed with Meat

Intact Meat is meat that has not been processed. (No tenderization, **communition** (cut, shredded, grounded, minced, etc,), or no vacuum tumbling)

Messed with Meat or Non-Intact Meat is meat that has been mechanically altered with a machine.
- Examples of messed with meat:
  - Ground turkey
  - Ground beef

- Cubed meat
- Mechanically tenderized meat
- Injected or brined meat
- Scored meat

Whether or not meat is intact or messed with, it should still be cooked to the correct temperature. (*Outlined in Section 6*)

Examples of Other TCS Foods include:
- Dairy
- Milk
- Eggs
- Baked Potatoes
- Tofu and soy products, meat alternatives
- **Cooked** Plant Food
  - Cooked Pasta
  - Cooked Beans
  - Cooked Rice

Temperature/Time Controlled for Safety (TCS) | Other Facts

- Cooked bacon can sit out for seven (7) days with no temperature control as long as there is no moisture.

- Food may be **reconditioned** if not held in the TDZ for more than two (2) hours.
  - *Ex: Hot dog chili may be reheated to the correct temperature if it was not in the TDZ for more than 2 hours.*

- The lower the pH value of a food, the higher the amount of acid in the food. Milk is more acidic than orange juice because milk has the lower pH value of the two. (Hard to believe, right?)

- Ceviche is a collection of seafood not made with heat. The acid from lime juice is used in ceviche in order to kill the pathogens in the seafood.

- **Lemon juice and lime juice** are commonly used to control pathogens in many foods.

Ready-to-Eat (RTE) Food

Ready-to-Eat (RTE) Food is food that is ready to be eaten without reheating, cooking, washing, thawing, and/or preparing prior to consumption.

Examples of RTE foods include:
- Precooked food
- Deli meat
- Whole or cut pre-washed fruit and vegetables
- Baked goods
- Packaged cookies or crackers
- Sandwiches, wraps, and tacos
- Sugar, salt, and seasonings

SECTION 2:
Safety/Sanitation

Food Safety Manager Study Guide Section 2 | Safety/Sanitation

Food Safety Managers are responsible for creating, implementing, and monitoring personal hygiene policies and procedures.

Handwashing Station

As mentioned in Section 1, handwashing is the best way to prevent foodborne illness. However, it must be done properly. It is important to remember that handwashing should only be allowed in a **sink designated for handwashing only**.

The **five (5)** requirements of a handwashing station are:
1. Hot and cold *potable (drinkable)* water
2. Soap
3. Single use/disposable paper towel (preferred) <u>or</u> way to dry hands
4. Garbage Container
5. Signage (Ex: Sign that says all employees must wash hands before returning to work.)

Handwashing stations ***are required in restrooms/right beside the restroom; and in food prep, service, and dishwashing areas.***

Complete Handwashing Process
- The process should take about 20 seconds
- Water should be **85°F**
- Apply soap
- Scrub for 10-15 seconds
- Rinse under running water
- Use a single use paper towel to dry hands
- Then use that same paper towel to turn off the faucet and to open the door

Why do you need to wash your hands?
- Feces/Fecal matter is on hands
- Feces/Fecal matter causes Hepatitis A and Norovirus, and other illnesses

When do you need to wash your hands?
- Before you start cooking
- After using the restroom or taking out the trash
- After touching animals (land or aquatic)
- When switching between foods
- After handling money
- After leaving the kitchen, then returning back to the kitchen
- After blowing your nose/using a tissue

- After sneezing or coughing
- After eating, drinking, smoking/vaping, using e-cigarettes, chewing gum

Other times when you need to wash your hands:
- When switching tasks
- Before putting on gloves
- After taking off gloves
- When changing gloves

Test Tip: You should only use single use gloves in the kitchen. Gloves should <u>not</u> be saved for later or reused.

Hand Sanitizers (Antiseptics)
- **Should only be used after washing hands or when you cannot wash your hands**
- <u>**Not**</u> a replacement for washing hands
- **Need to be FDA approved**
- Need to be **at least 60% alcohol**
- When using hand sanitizer, you should use enough that your hands are soaking and **take at least 15 seconds to completely dry**

Other Important Hand Hygiene Facts
- **Always wash hands before putting on gloves**
- Use a Band-Aid and glove or Band-Aid and finger cot if you have a cut on your hand
- Wounds and boils should be covered with a waterproof/**impermeable** dressing that is **durable and tight-fitting**, <u>and</u> a glove must be worn over the dressing
- Gloves are required if you have on nail polish (some restaurants may have a no polish at all policy)
- Fake nails should not be worn, damaged nails should be cleaned/trimmed
- <u>**Smooth plain band ring**</u> is the only jewelry allowed in the kitchen (no diamonds, cuts should be on rings, and you should not wear earrings, necklaces, bracelets (including medical bracelets), etc.)
- **Never handle RTE (Ready-to-Eat) food with bare hands**
  - Use spatulas, tongs, deli sheets, etc.
  - Clean utensils prior to use

Test Tip: Gloves <u>**are not**</u> required when:
1. Washing produce
2. Foods will be properly cooked
   > Ex: When dressing a pizza in a restaurant because pizza ovens are really hot (450° or higher) and will kill germs

Gloves should not be:
- Ripped/torn
- Blown into or rolled prior to putting them on
- Too big or too tight

Proper Attire/Clothing in the Kitchen

All food handlers should wear:
1. Clean Apron (Should be removed before going to the bathroom)
2. Hat/Hair Net
3. Beard Guard **(if beard is longer than ¼")**

Food handlers should also **wear closed-toe and slip-resistant shoes.**

False eyelashes are also not allowed in the kitchen as they can be a physical contaminant.

Drinks in the Kitchen

Beverages should:
1. Have a lid and a straw
2. Have a name on the container
3. Be stored on bottom shelf or away from food prep areas

Saliva in the Kitchen

Saliva and germs from our bodies could potentially contaminate food.

While in the kitchen/food prep areas:
- No smoking
- No drinking
- No eating from an open container
- No chewing gum

*Test Tip: Smoking and using tobacco products in the kitchen is not acceptable, **but smoking and using tobacco products in designated areas outside is acceptable.**

Break areas should also be strategically located in an establishment to prevent the risk of food contamination in the kitchen.

Handing Sick Employees

Restrict employees with:
- Sore Throat
- Fever
- Improperly covered wounds or boils
- Runny noses, sneezing and coughing symptoms

Exclude employees with:
- Vomiting
- Diarrhea
- Jaundice

Restrict Vs. Exclude

Restricted food handlers can work in the operation, but they cannot work around food.

Excluded food handlers **cannot come to work at all**. They <u>must stay at home</u>.

What is Jaundice?
- Condition characterized by **yellowing** of the skin or eyes
- **Symptom/Indicator of Hepatitis A** (a disease that affects the **liver**)
- Food handler **must be excluded** from work
- Contact the health department **(State and Local Regulatory Authority)** immediately

To return to work after a Jaundice diagnosis:
- Food handler must be symptom-free for at least 24 hours **and**
- Cleared by a doctor with a note

Highly Susceptible Population (HSP)

There are some groups of people that are more likely to be affected by foodborne illness than others. These Highly Susceptible Populations (HSPs) are identified using the **YOPI acronym**.

Young
Old
Pregnant
Immunocompromised (Ex: Sick people, hospital patients, cancer patients, dialysis recipients, etc.)

*Test tip: A person must be excluded from work if they work with a **YOPI** population and **have any type of illness** because these populations do not have strong immune systems.

The Big Six (6) Pathogens

While there are many pathogens that cause foodborne illness, the FDA has defined six of these pathogens as highly infectious. These six pathogens are known as **The Big Six**. The Big Six Pathogens include:

Salmonella **(Regular and Typhi/Typhoid)**
Hepatitis A
E. Coli
Norovirus
Shigella

Use the acronym SHENS to remember these pathogens.

SHENS illnesses are highly contagious because they are transmitted through the **fecal-oral** route.

> **Fecal-oral transmission** occurs when the food handler has feces on their hands, and they touch food and other surfaces with those hands; and someone then eats the contaminated food or from the contaminated surface.

Test Tip: If someone has a SHENS diagnosis in your restaurant or establishment:
- Exclude them from the operation
- Contact the health department immediately

CAUSES OF THE BIG SIX (6) PATHOGENS

Salmonella: raw and undercooked poultry and eggs
Hepatitis A: Feces, bad shellfish, and RTE foods
E. Coli: Animal feces like cow intestines, meat contaminated during slaughtering
Norovirus: RTE foods, feces, and bad shellfish
Shigella: Feces from food and water, feces carried by flies

Note: Among the SHENS illnesses, **Hepatitis A and Norovirus** are <u>two of the most contagious</u> foodborne illnesses.

It is also important to note that **Hepatitis A is not destroyed by normal cooking temperatures.**

Test tip: Hepatitis B and Hepatitis C have **nothing** to do with foodborne illness. (*A question about this is sometimes thrown in on the test to trick you.*)

Symptoms of foodborne illness may include:
- Diarrhea
- Nausea
- Vomiting
- Stomach cramps
- Fever
- Death

Symptoms may show up in a few minutes or they may take weeks to appear.

Note: Sometimes people can carry infections unknowingly. Someone who does this is known as a carrier. A **carrier** is someone who carries infections, *but they do not have any symptoms.*

OTHER FACTS ABOUT SICK EMPLOYEES

Restaurants need written procedures for handling vomit & diarrhea when customers, employees, or staff get sick. **This is required to minimize the potential for spreading illnesses.**

An *Employee Health Policy Agreement* must be in place in every establishment. Basically, this document says that if you or someone in your household has a SHENS diagnosis or is sick, you will let management know ASAP.

SECTION 3:
Facility/Equipment

The use of proper equipment in an establishment is also very important in preventing foodborne illness.

Floors, Walls, and Ceilings

Floors, walls, and ceilings should be:
- Smooth
- Durable
- Easy to clean

Floor coving should be installed where the floor and wall meet because it reduces sharpness, is easier to clean, and makes it easy to sweep.

Lighting

Proper lighting is required for cleaning and safety. Employees need to be able to see properly in order to work properly.

Lighting in a commercial kitchen should have the following:
- Protective shield or
- Protective lens

Ventilation

Proper ventilation and cooktop/oven hoods are required to prevent the buildup of grease and moisture.

Excessive grease and moisture in a kitchen can lead to employee health issues, equipment problems, pest infestations, and grease fires.

Water Supply and Sinks:

Only safe/potable water should be used to prepare food as this helps to prevent foodborne illness.

It is also very important that facilities are designed to prevent a cross-connection in the plumbing system.

What is a cross-connection?

A cross-connection is a physical link between a **safe and unsafe water** source. When a cross-connection occurs, safe water comes into contact with contaminated water.

- *Other terms for "Safe and Unsafe" include*:
  - Potable and Non-Potable
  - Drinkable and Undrinkable

Cross-connections often occur around **drains, sewers, and sources of wastewater.**

Back-flow or back-siphonage

Back-flow or back-siphonage is a prime example of a cross-connection.

Back-flow or back-siphonage occurs when water flows in **reverse due to a change in pressure** within the plumbing system.

- Example I: A faucet hangs below the flood rim of the sink. The running water from the faucet comes into contact with dishwater in the sink causing a cross-connection.

- Example II: A hose is left running in a bucket. An increase in pressure in the bucket pushes contaminated water back into the hose causing a cross-connection.

Note: The only guaranteed way to prevent back-flow/back-siphonage is by making sure that an air-gap is present.

An **air gap** is the space between where the water comes out of the faucet/fixture and the flood rim of the sink. Water has no way of flowing back into the air and into the faucet. *It is literally impossible for this to occur.*

Another way to prevent back-flow/back-siphonage is with the use of **vacuum breakers** on a faucet. Vacuum breakers only allow water to flow in one direction thus preventing back-flow/back-siphonage.

Test Tip: If you put a hose at the end of a faucet, then you must use a vacuum breaker in order to prevent back-flow/back-siphonage.

Grease traps should also be used in commercial kitchen sinks to prevent grease from blocking drains. Blocked drains can cause water backups, flooding, water damage, etc. All of which are health and safety hazards.

Kitchen Equipment

Kitchen equipment must be approved by:
National Sanitation Foundation **(NSF)**
American National Standards Institute **(ANSI)**
- National Accreditation Board **(ANAB)**

Look for the following marks on equipment to demonstrate certification of sanitation:
- NSF mark
- UL EPH classified mark
- ETL sanitation mark

Kitchen Equipment must be:
- Smooth
- Durable
- Easy to clean
- Resistant to Damage

Floor equipment in the kitchen must be:
- **Six (6) inches off of the floor**
- **On casters/wheels** (making it easier to move)
- **Mounted** to the floor if not on wheels (prevents health and safety hazards)
  - Food, dirt/debris, insects/rodents **cannot get under equipment that is mounted to the floor.**

Following these guidelines for floor equipment prevents safety hazards, but doing so also prevents health hazards; resulting in a kitchen that is safe and easy to clean.

Counter equipment in the kitchen must be:
- **Four (4) inches off the countertop** to help with pest control/pest prevention.

Pest Prevention

In addition to cleaning and sanitizing the kitchen often, it is very important that the Food Safety Manager remembers the "Three (3) NOs of Pest Prevention.

1. No **Food**
2. No **Water**
3. No Shelter/**Harborage** (no space for the bugs to live)

In a nutshell, keep things neat, clean, and dry. Put food away, make sure floors are swept, and make sure that all surface areas are free of food, crumbs, etc.

Test Tip: Deny food, water, and shelter/harborage to prevent pest infestation in the commercial kitchen.**Ways to Prevent Pest Infestation:**

In addition to denying pests food, water, and shelter/harborage, establishments can do the following to prevent pests:

1. Install air curtains that blow to prevent pests/insects from coming inside
2. Inspect food shipments immediately for signs of pest infestation
3. Install screens within the facility and seal outside openings where pests can enter

If the PIC notices that there is a pest problem, they should contact a **Licensed Pest Control operator** as soon as possible.

Garbage Containers

Indoor garbage cans must be:
- **Leakproof**
- **Waterproof**
- **Easy to clean**

Outdoor garbage cans must:
- **Have tight fitting lids**
- **Be sitting on concrete/asphalt (nonabsorbent surface)**

Note: Do not clean garbage containers near food storage or prep areas. That is unsanitary and it is unsafe!

SECTION 4:
Cleaning & Sanitizing

Food Safety Manager Study Guide Section 4 | Cleaning & Sanitizing

It is important to clean and sanitize the commercial kitchen on a routine basis in order to prevent foodborne illness.

The general recommendation is that the kitchen should be cleaned and sanitized **every four (4) hours** for continual use.

However, equipment and utensils should be washed, rinsed, and sanitized after each use regardless of how much time has passed between usage,

What is the difference between cleaning and sanitizing?

Cleaning removes dirt and debris.

> **Clean** general surfaces like:
> - Walls
> - Floors
> - Storage Shelves
> - Garbage Containers

Sanitizing reduces pathogens to safe levels.

> **Sanitize** food surfaces like:
> - Prep Tables and Countertops
> - Knives
> - Meat Cutters

As you can see, **food contact surfaces must be sanitized**. Everything else in the kitchen can just be cleaned.

Test Tip: Butcher equipment and equipment in a cold environment may be cleaned and sanitized every 24 hours.

The 5-Step Process for Cleaning & Sanitizing Equipment and Utensils

To help cut down on the risk of contamination in the kitchen, restaurants should follow the 5-Step Process in the following order:
1. Scrape or remove food
2. Wash
3. Rinse
4. Sanitize (Use chemicals or hot water)
5. Air-Dry

Note: Using a cloth to dry dishes is **not recommended** as this can create and/or spread bacteria.

Sanitizing with Chemicals

When sanitizing with chemicals, it is important to know the following concentrations and contact time for each chemical listed below. Use test strips to measure the **concentration/strength** of the sanitizer in ppm (parts per million).

Chlorine/Bleach	Iodine	Quats (Ammonia Based)
50-99 ppm	12.5-25 ppm	Manufacturer Recommendations
7 seconds	30 seconds	30 seconds

SAFETY TIP: NEVER mix chlorine and bleach. It could kill you!
Your business should only use one or the other. And they should not be in the same building at the same time.

Factors that affect the effectiveness of sanitizer:
1. Concentration
2. Temperature
3. Contact Time
4. pH
5. Water Hardness

Sanitizing with Hot Water

When sanitizing with hot water, it is important to know the correct order of cleaning and sanitizing using a **3-compartment sink**. The 3-compartment sink should be organized as follows:

Sink 1: Detergent and Hot Water
Sink 2: Clean Water
Sink 3: Water and Sanitizer
The hot water used in the sink should be 110°F.

Test Tip: You must wash, rinse, and sanitize all three (3) sinks **before** starting the 5-step process; and the wash water needs to be at least **110°F.**

Test Tip: A dishwashing/sanitizing machine may also be used for dishes, cookware, dinnerware, utensils, etc. Unlike the other processes that use water to sanitize, **the wash water temperature should be 180°F** when using a dishwasher/sanitizer.

Master Cleaning Schedule

A Master Cleaning Schedule is a document/plan that lists in detail all of the required cleaning tasks of an establishment. This schedule shows:
- Who cleans
- What needs to be cleaned
- When and how it should be cleaned

Ex: Who is going to clean the shelves, clean the fans, clean the refrigerator, clean the stove, etc?

A Master Cleaning Schedule is an example of a Standard Operating Procedure (SOP). **Standard Operating Procedures (SOPs)** are written instructions on how to perform a routine business activity.

Having SOPs in place for cleaning/sanitizing will help cut down on threats to food safety in the establishment.

Creating a Master Cleaning Schedule

When creating a Master Cleaning Schedule it is important to:
1. Keep it simple
2. Require general food safety training for all staff
3. Train staff on how to follow schedule (requires initial and ongoing training)
4. Monitor the program to make sure it is effective

Test Tip: As a Food Safety Manager, you do not need to hire an outside company to clean your business. You and your employees can do it effectively as long as you all are adhering to the Master Cleaning Schedule.

Mop Sinks

Mop sinks are also known as *service sinks*. These sinks should never be used for preparing food, handwashing, etc. These sinks are specifically designed with floor drains for use when cleaning mops and other floor cleaning tools, and pouring out mop water.

When not in use, mops and brooms should be hanging. Mops **should not** touch the floor or be left in a bucket. **This allows for bacteria, mold, and other pathogens to grow.**

Other Cleaning and Sanitizing Facts

- **Employees should have access to cleaning products at all times**
  - Cleaning products should be:
    - Stable
    - Non-corrosive
    - Safe to Use

- Unplug equipment prior to cleaning, then wash, rinse, and sanitize removable parts and food contact surfaces, then air-dry these parts/surfaces

- Dirty linens should be placed in a **dirty linen bag**
  - They should not be left out in the open

- Sanitizer buckets should be **below** the work table and **6 inches** of the floor

- Cleaning and/or sanitizer solution should be **changed every 4 hours**

- Cloths should be left in the cleaning and/or sanitizer bucket between uses

SECTION 5:
Receiving & Storing

Food Safety Manager Study Guide Section 5 | Receiving & Storing

It is important to receive and store food properly in order to prevent foodborne illness.

Purchasing Food From Suppliers

All food including mushrooms, plants, and seafood should be purchased from approved and reputable suppliers.

Test Tip: The responsibility for managing food safety **begins with** approved food purchasing.

Food Suppliers need to be:
- Approved
- Reputable

Food prepared in someone's home is **not reputable, and it is generally considered unsafe**.

> However, *food donations are allowed* in some instances. Food donation is acceptable when food has been:
> - **Held** according to the Food Code
> - **Prepared** according to the Food Code
> - **Packaged** according to the Food Code

Commercially Raised Food

- **Game animals (deer) must be commercially raised for food**
  - Commercially raised food is food that was raised in controlled and confined areas
- Farm raised fish must have documentation that shows it was raised according to FDA policies
- Mushrooms must come from approved **foragers** to control toxins found in certain mushrooms
- Wild animals are not approved for establishments

Shellstock Identification Tags

Shellstock identification tags are required for shellfish (clams, mussels, oysters) delivered to a restaurant by a supplier.

These tags need to be kept for **90 days** after the last item has been sold or served from the bag.

Why 90 days? 90 days is the **incubation period** for Hepatitis A (linked to bad shellfish).

Test Tip: Fish packaged using Reduced Oxygen Packaging (ROP) must be frozen to control parasites. This fish must also have a label on it that states that the fish must be frozen until used.

Receiving Food

When receiving food, it is important to:

- Inspect it immediately upon receipt
- Correctly accept or reject deliveries. Look for signs of:
    - Thawing and refreezing (time-temperature abuse)
    - Pest
    - Expired dates
    - Dented/rusted or leaky cans
    - Missing labels
    - Dirty or damaged packaging or seals
    - Signs of tampering
- Follow food safety handling policies at all times
- Store items correctly as soon as possible

Handling Damaged Items

When handling damaged items:

- **Remove** the items from inventory
- Label them **DO NOT USE AND DO NOT DISCARD**
- **Reject** the items and **return** them to the supplier

Receiving Food After Hours

Sometimes food is delivered when the establishment is closed by way of a **key drop delivery**. Key drop deliveries:

- Occur after hours
- Require the food supplier to have a key to the operation
- Require the delivery driver to put food in its **proper storage location**
- Require staff to inspect deliveries when they arrive to the establishment

Delivered Items Linked to a Foodborne Illness Outbreak

Sometimes previously delivered food will be found to be a source of foodborne illness. If this ever occurs:
- Remove food from inventory
- Separate from other food
- Label "Do not discard and do not use"
- Follow vendor's recall instructions (throw it out or return it)

Exceptions to the Delivery Temperature Rule

Eggs, shellstock (live molluscan shellfish like oysters, mussels, and clams), shucked molluscan shellfish (shellfish with both shells removed), and milk can be delivered with a temperature up to **45°F**, but must be cooled to **41°F** within four (4) hours.

Thermometers

Proper use of thermometers is important in the commercial kitchen. Using thermometers correctly will aid in preventing time and temperature abuse.

Thermometers:
- Need to be **+/-2°** to be accurate
- Need to have **easy to read** markings
- Need to be cleaned and sanitized **before and after** each use
- Calibrated often (adjusted so that it reads correctly)
  - Thermometers should also be calibrated again if bumped or dropped
  - **Cold/ice water calibration** is the best way to get an accurate temperature reading
    - The process of cold/ice water calibration involves sticking the thermometer in cold/ice water. (*If the thermometer is reading a really high temperature, then you know the thermometer is inaccurate because cold/ice water will never be hot.*)

Types of Thermometers

Bimetallic stemmed thermometer
- Measures temperature through a metal stem

Penetration Probe
- Used to check the **internal temperature** of foods like hamburger patties

Immersion Probe
- Used to check the temperature of **liquids**

Surface Probe
- Used for checking the temperature of **flat** cooking equipment like a **griddle**

Air Probe
- Used for checking the temperature inside a **cooler or oven**

Infrared (laser) thermometer
- Used to measure the **surface temperature** of food and equipment

Maximum registering thermometer
- Used to check the highest temperature reached during use

Time-temperature indicators (TTI)
- Measure time and temperature
- Change colors when they recognize time-temperature abuse

Other Thermometer Facts:
- Test oven thermometers in the coolest place in the oven
  - If the coolest place in the oven is hot enough, then the other areas will automatically be hot enough
- Test cooler thermometers in the warmest place in the cooler
  - If the warmest place in the cooler is cold enough, then the other areas will automatically be cold enough

An **ambient hanging thermometer** should be hung in the warmest part of the walk-in storage cooler to ensure the cooler is cold enough.

Storing Food

All food stored in an establishment should be properly labeled.

Here are a few important things to remember when labeling food before storing it:
- Label dry goods with a **common name** (Ex: Label should read flour, sugar, salt, etc.)
- Items like **Homemade Ranch** should be used within 24 hours and can have a label with a common name
- **Food kept for more than 24 hours** should have a common name and a **discard date**

How Long Can Food Be Stored?

- **Food can be kept in the refrigerator for seven (7) days**. After the seven days have passed, the food must be discarded.

What is the formula for determining the discard date of an item?

Date the Item was Made + 6 days = 7 days
Ex: Soup cooked on June 2nd must be discarded on June 8th.
(June 2 + 6 days = June 8)

When to Throw Items With Multiple Ingredients Away

Example: For this example, we will use potato salad made by a restaurant on September 2nd.

Ingredients Used: Mustard that expires on September 8th
Mayonnaise that expires on September 7th
Eggs that expire September 4th

When should you throw the potato salad out? Answer: September 4th

Why? Because you should always pay attention to the **expiration dates** of **all** of the ingredients used to make the dish. **The expiration date of the first ingredient to expire should be used as the discard date.**

Food Storage Locations

When storing food, it is very important to store food in food storage areas only.

Never store food in:

- Machine or boiler rooms
- Locker rooms
- Near sewer of leaky water lines
- Restrooms
- Trash areas
- Underneath staircases

Examples of what not to do when storing food:
- Do not store flour on the floor
- Do not put dish detergent next to food items
- Do not store sugar in an unlabeled container
- Discard cans that have rust, dents, or bulging/swollen ends

- Do not line shelves with aluminum foil, sheet pans, or paper
  - **Using these items will restrict air circulation, and could cause the food to spoil.**

FIFO Method for Storage (First In, First Out)

The FIFO Method is one of the best ways to keep food safe.

- Foods cooked first go in front of foods that were cooked later.
- This applies to the refrigerator and the dry storage/pantry areas as well.

When correctly using the FIFO method, you will automatically know that items in the front of the storage area expire before the items in the back of the storage area.

Safe Refrigerator Storage Order

Knowing how to store items properly in the refrigerator also plays an important role in food safety. Items more likely to contaminate other items will go on the bottom shelves of the refrigerator. The proper way to store items in the refrigerator is as follows from **top to bottom:**

1. Top Shelf: RTE Foods
2. Seafood
3. Chops/Filets/Steaks
4. Ground Meat
5. Bottom Shelf: Poultry

Test Tip: As an **exception,** ground meat and ground fish may be stored on top of whole cuts of chops/filets/steaks as long as the package does not leak and it is designed to keep out pathogens and chemicals.

SECTION 6:
Preparing & Serving

Food Safety Manager Study Guide Section 6 | Preparing & Serving

It is important to prepare and serve food properly in order to prevent foodborne illness.

Minimum Internal Cooking Temperatures

Making sure that food is cooked to the correct minimum internal cooking temperatures helps to ensure that harmful bacteria is killed in the food; and it also cuts down on the risk of foodborne illness.

Listed below you will find the Minimum Internal Cooking Temperatures of food items based on **Safe Refrigerator Storage Order**.

135° F: RTE Foods (No minimum)
145° F: Seafood (15 seconds)
145° F: Chops/Filets/Steaks (15 seconds)
155° F: Ground Meat (17 seconds)
165° F: Poultry | Whole or ground chicken, turkey, duck (1 second, instantaneous)

- Instantaneous means that bacteria and pathogens will be killed as soon as the temperature reaches **165° F.** It <u>does not mean</u> that it only takes 1 second to cook poultry.

It is important to note that **minimum internal cooking temperatures must be held for at least the number of seconds indicated next to the item in order to kill pathogens like bacteria and viruses.** *This does not mean that the food items will be completely cooked and done in the number of seconds listed.*

Other Minimum Internal Cooking Temperatures

135°F: RTE foods like fruits, vegetables, pasta, rice held for hot service (15 seconds)

145°F: Over medium eggs, and eggs that will be immediately served (15 seconds)
145°F: Commercially raised game (15 seconds)

145°F: Pork roast, beef roast, veal roast, lamb roast (4 minutes)

155°F: Buffet Eggs, Mechanically Tenderized Meat (17 seconds)
155°F: Vacuum-tumbled meats with marinade (17 seconds)
155°F: Cubed or Pounded Meat (17 seconds)
155°F: Meat from commercially raised game animals (17 seconds)
155°F: Ground, chopped, or minced seafood (17 seconds)

165°F: Anything stuffed, anything with 2 or more ingredients, anything microwaved (1 second, instantaneous)
165°F: Food items that contain previously cooked TCS ingredients
165°F: Reheating Foods | 165°F must be reached within 2 hours. **(Make sure you throw away uneaten reheated food.** You should not reheat food twice.)

Test Tip: Employees should be monitoring food temperatures very closely at all times. They should also be trained on what corrective active steps need to be taken if food items do not meet temperature requirements. **Temperatures should be checked every two (2) hours to allow time for corrective action.**

Checking Temperature While Cooking

When cooking food, always check the temperature in the **thickest part** of the food. **Why?** Because thinner parts cook faster and you need to make sure the food is completely done.

Parcooking occurs when food is partially cooked during preparation. When parcooking, the establishment should:
- Not cook the food longer than 60 minutes
- Refrigerate or freeze the food after cooling it
- Hold food at **41°F or lower,** and hold it away from RTE food
- Cook food to the correct minimum internal cooking temperature before serving
- Have approval from the state and local regulatory authority to parcook food

Manufacturer Cooking Instructions

- Prior to adding certain foods to RTE dishes, establishments must prepare packaged food according to the manufactures instructions on the label
- Ex: If a restaurant wants to use packaged/frozen corn on their salad bar, **they must first cook the corn according to the instructions on the package**, then cool it down before placing it on the salad bar

Consumer Advisory

Menus must include a Consumer Advisory. (Usually found at the bottom or back of a menu.)

A Consumer Advisory warns about the risk of eating raw, undercooked, and cooked-to-order foods.
  - *Example: Consuming raw or undercooked meats, poultry, seafood, shellfish, or eggs may increase your risk of foodborne illness, especially if you have certain medical conditions.*

Cooling Food

In addition to being properly cooked, food must also be properly cooled in order to remain safe. When cooling food:

Food must go from:
135°F to 70°F within 2 hours

Then from:
70°F to 41°F within 4 hours

Total Cooling Time: 6 hours

Food must be properly cooled before putting it in the cooler/refrigerator.

Note: Yes, six (6) hours is correct! Even considering what you learned about the Temperature Danger Zone (TDZ). **However, it is recommended that food is cooled quickly and properly to avoid keeping food in the TDZ too long.**

Note: Restaurants are required to keep a **cooldown log** to show that food was properly cooled. The cooldown log will show temperatures at every hour of the cooling process. It will also show corrective actions that were taken, if applicable.

Methods for Cooling Down Food

There are various methods that can be used to cool food to include:

- Smaller portions (Separate containers)
    - Ex: A large pot of soup takes longer to cool than a small pot of soup so putting soup in smaller containers will make it cool faster
- Ice water bath
    - Placing the food container in a container/bucket of ice
- Ice paddles
    - A plastic container filled with water, and then frozen
    - The container is then used to stir food
- Blast chiller
    - Equipment used to cool food fast
    - A specialized freezer that uses forced cool air to lower temperature
- Ice as an ingredient
    - Ex: Adding ice to soup, but using less liquid upfront to cook the soup since the ice will melt creating more liquid in the soup
- Shallow Stainless Steel Containers
    - Shallow containers cool faster than deep containers

Cook Chill Food

Food establishments are allowed to cook a TCS food product, store it in Reduced Oxygen Packaging (ROP), and immediately chill it down. During the cook chill process food must be either:

1. Cooled to **34°F within 48 hours of reaching 41°F** and held in ROP at the temperature until consumed within seven (7) days, but no more than thirty (30) days from the date of packaging **or**
2. Frozen with no shelf life time limit until consumed

Approved Ways to Thaw Meats

There are various methods that can be used to thaw meats to include:

- Using running water not above **70°F**
- Placing items in the refrigerator
- Microwaving
  - Note: Food must be cooked immediately after microwaving since cooking has started
- As part of the cooking process
  - Frozen to pan/cooking directly from frozen

Test Tip: Never thaw meat on the countertop and/or at room temperature as this is unsafe!

When thawing food, food should **never be held over 41°F** for more than four (4) hours.

Test Tip: Frozen fish in Reduced Oxygen Packaging (ROP) should be thawed in the refrigerator to cut down on the risk of **botulism**.

Cross-Contamination

Cross-contamination is a common threat to food safety. **Cross-contamination** is the transfer of harmful bacteria from one food to another.

To cut down on the risk of cross-contamination, food/meals should be prepped in the order that it goes in the refrigerator.

    Ex. Prepare a salad before preparing chicken.

Always remember to **wash, rinse, and sanitize** equipment in between prepping different types of food.

Avoiding Cross-Contamination

Some ways to avoid cross-contamination include:

Washing produce before cutting it
Wearing gloves (Wash hands first)
Changing utensils and gloves between each use
Avoiding preparing items near allergens
Setting up different areas of kitchen for preparing different foods
Concentrating on prepping one food at a time
Keeping workstations cleaned and/or sanitized
Being mindful when restocking work stations
Separating raw food from RTE fruits and vegetables at all times
Using different equipment for raw food and RTE food
- Try to prepare RTE food first

Color Coded Cutting Boards

Using color coded cutting boards also cuts down on the risk of cross-contamination. Listed below you will find the cutting board color next to its corresponding food item.

Yellow: Poultry
Red: Pork/Meat
Green: Produce
Blue: Seafood
White: Dairy Products
Brown: Cooked Foods
Purple: Allergy Foods

Food Allergies

Cross-contact is another common threat to food safety. **Cross-contact** occurs when one food allergen comes in contact with another food item.

Ex: Almonds/nuts prepped with same utensils or beside lettuce for a salad, or using the same cooking oil for different foods

A **food allergen** is a protein in a food or ingredient that can cause an allergic reaction in some people when consumed.

Test Tip: Management or **Person in Charge (PIC)** and serving staff need to know the ingredients in every dish, even secret sauces because customers have food allergies. While the owner may not want to give their secret away, *the customer always has the right to know what is in the "secret sauce"*.

The BIG 9 Food Allergens (Most common food allergens according to the FDA)

1. Peanuts
2. Tree Nuts
3. Milk
4. Eggs
5. Wheat
6. Soybeans (soy)
7. Fish
8. Shellfish
9. Sesame

The Big 9 allergens are known to cause 9 out of 10 allergic reactions.

Food Allergy Symptoms

It is important to note that food allergy symptoms may occur over time or **within minutes.** Food allergy symptoms may include:

- Hives
- Rash
- Swelling
- Hot and Cold Sensations
- Tingling Sensations
- Burning in Mouth
- Heart Palpitations
- Wheezing/Trouble Breathing
- Cardiac
- **Anaphylactic Shock (most severe/may lead to death)**
- Death

Act fast if someone tells you that they are experiencing food allergy symptoms. You never know how serious their symptoms may be, and you do not want to take any chances.

Test Tip: Employees (both front of house staff and back of house staff) need to be properly trained on allergy awareness.

Employees should know all food allergens in order to prevent allergic reactions; and they should be able to spot an allergic reaction immediately.

Front of House Staff are the first point of contact for customers. They really need to understand the importance of working with customers with food allergies so that they can know how to properly tell guests about the menu, receive orders from guests with food allergies, and properly place special orders for guests with food allergies.

Pasteurized Food

Pasteurized eggs should be used in nursing homes for all dishes, and pasteurized eggs should be used in homemade ranch dressing regardless of the establishment.

   Pasteurization is a process that reduces the risk of foodborne illness. Eggs are cooked briefly at a high temperature and then cooled.

Test Tip: Nursing homes/daycares should use pasteurized eggs because they serve the YOPI population. They should also not serve unpasteurized juice, raw and/or undercooked food, and frozen vegetables that have not been cooked according to the manufacturer's instructions prior to serving. ***This is because those a part of the YOPI population typically do not have a strong immune system***; and they are more likely to get sick than others.

Prepared Foods/Grab and Go Foods

Packaged food ingredients should be listed on labels:
   - **In descending order by weight.** (Highest to lowest)

   Big 9 Food Allergens must also be clearly listed. *(Ex: This product contains wheat.)*

Serving Food in Establishments

Food must be **honestly presented** at sit-down restaurants, buffets, and for catering. **No food coloring**. No misleading. Customers need to know what they will be consuming.

Allergens must also be listed on menus. Staff should be aware of all ingredients in items on the menu so that they can inform customers about what different dishes are made from.

Staff should also confirm that they are serving people with allergies correctly. The ordered meal must match what is on the ticket prior to serving. This is done to prevent the customer from coming in contact with their known allergen.

Serving Prepackaged/Unopened Food

Prepackaged/unopened food may be served from one table to another.

     Ex: Ketchup packets and crackers from Table A can be given to Table B as long as they have not been opened.

Serving Food to the Same Table

Bread baskets may be refilled/reused without sanitizing, **but should be changed between guests/tables**.

     Ex: A waitress can continuously bring multiple bread basket refills back to the same table as long as the guests are the same, but once those guests leave and new guests sit down, then a completely new bread basket must be used.

Buffets and Self-Serve Areas

In order to ensure food safety in buffet and self-serve areas, it is important to remember that:

- Every item needs its own utensil and label
- Sneeze guards are required
- Employees need to monitor self-service areas
- Raw meat should be kept separate from RTE food (Ex: Raw shrimp on a salad bar should not be near lettuce)
- Bakery items do not require a label
- Signage is required (*Ex: Customers need a clean plate each trip to buffet bar.*)

Dogs in Outdoor Serving Areas

Dogs (both pet and service animals) are now allowed on outdoor patios and in other other dining areas as allowed by the establishment.

Other Facts About Serving Food

- An insulated **food-grade container** with a label is required any time an establishment is transporting food off-site
  - Internal temperatures should also be checked regularly

- Items like coleslaw can sit out for up to six (6) hours without refrigeration as long as the temperature does not go above **70°F**
  - **The item must have been held at 41°F or lower prior to removing it from refrigeration**
  - Item must have a label detailing the time it was removed from refrigeration, and time it must be thrown away

- ○ Item must be sold, served, or thrown away within six (6) hours

- Hot food at a catered event can be left out without temperature control for up to 4 hours

- Raw/unpackaged meat can be offered up for self-service when it will be cooked and eaten immediately

- Ice used to keep food cold should never be used to prepare drinks

- Take home food containers may be used if they are provided by the restaurant, and may only be reused if they are designed for reuse

- Take home beverage containers can be refilled if the beverage is not a TCS food, and if the container is for the same guest
  - ○ Container should be rinsed with hot water before refilling
  - ○ Guests may also refill their beverage containers if a contamination prevention method is present

- Uncovered condiments (ex: open ketchup mini-cups) should not be re-served
  - ○ Leftover condiments should not be combined with new, fresh condiments

Clearing Tables After Customers Leave

When clearing or bussing tables, it is important to remember to:

- Hold silverware by middle not mouthpiece
- Hold cups/glassware by base or middle, or use a rack
  - ○ Do not stack glasses and carry them under face and/or on your body
- **Clean and sanitize unused utensils, even if they appear unwrapped**

Equipment to Avoid

It is important that an establishment does not use equipment made from lead, pewter, copper, and zinc. This equipment **may chemically react with highly acidic foods like orange juice and tomato juice,** thus making the customer sick if they eat contaminated food prepared using this equipment.

SECTION 7:
Keeping Food Safe

Food Safety Manager Study Guide Section 7 | Keeping Food Safe

Active Managerial Control

The Food Safety Manager plays a major role in keeping food safe within an establishment. As the Food Safety Manager, you must always remember that you are the Person in Charge.

The Person in Charge (PIC) must:
a. Be a Certified Food Protection Manager
  - Must show they have knowledge by passing a test from a program accredited by the Conference for Food Protection
b. Be onsite all day while the establishment is operating

However, markets **without cashiers and convenience stores may not require** a PIC onsite at all times if the state and local authority recognizes the establishment as low risk for foodborne illness.

As a Person in Charge (PIC), you are responsible for managing and monitoring your kitchen, and preventing the five (5) most common risk factors for foodborne illness to include:

1. Purchasing food from unsafe sources
2. Failing to cook food correctly
3. Holding food at incorrect/improper temperatures
4. Using contaminated equipment
5. Poor personal hygiene

Managers are responsible for making sure all staff members know and follow all food safety practices/procedures by way of **identifying risks, constant monitoring, taking corrective action, training staffing, overseeing the staff, and re-evaluating policies/procedures when necessary**. All staff training should also be documented upon completion.

An effective Food Safety Manager is highly capable of maintaining **Active Managerial Control**. A well-qualified Food Safety manager also has excellent systems in place for *monitoring the flow of food to include*:
  - Food Safety Training
  - Personal Hygiene
  - Supplier Selection and Requirements
  - Quality Control and Assurance
  - Cleaning and Sanitizing
  - Standard Operating Procedures (SOPs)

- Facility Design and Equipment
- Pest Control

State and Local Regulatory Authority

The # 1 job of the State and Local Regulatory Authority is to protect the general public. The State and Local Regulatory Authority:
- Is commonly known as the Health Department
- Writes or issues codes for retail and foodservice establishments
- Inspects operations, and enforces regulations
- Issues permits/licenses
- Investigate foodborne illness claims or instances
- Issues variances

A key player in food safety that is employed by/works for the Health Department is the Health Inspector. **The Health Inspector is responsible for regularly checking up on the food establishment to make sure it is in compliance with the Health Department's rules and regulations**.

With so many threats to food safety in this day and time, it is important to make sure the Health Inspector properly identifies themself when they visit the establishment. It is perfectly fine to request to see a Health Inspector's ID/badge before they enter the kitchen.

Hazard Analysis Critical Control Point (HACCP) Plan

When preparing food outside of the food code, establishments must have a written Hazard Analysis Critical Control Point (HACCP) plan in place.

HACCP plans:
- Gives the establishment permission to cook food outside of the food code
- Are used to identify risks of contamination at specific points in the flow of food preparation
- Are required when applying for variances

HACCPs are unique to the specific business because every establishment operates differently.

Variances

Variances are needed when using different equipment, facilities, or cooking methods other than what is found in the food code. *The state and local regulatory issues variances that permit the establishment to change or waive policies for preparing food.*

Examples of when a variance is required:
- ROP- Reduced Oxygen Packaging (used to keep raw meat safe and fresh)
- Curing meat and smoking food
- Sprouting beans
- Using food additives to preserve (Ex: using vinegar)
- Cook & Rapid Chill
- Canning & Pickling
- Displaying live mollusk and shellfish in a tank
- Pasteurizing juice on site

An HACCP is required when applying for a variance because:
- The plan must show how the establishment will handle food safety threats
- The plan must show how the establishment will monitor and adhere to the plan

If a variance is granted, it must be on record at the establishment at all times.

Imminent Health Hazards

An **imminent health hazard** is a condition or situation that can cause significant harm, illness, injury, or death to the general public.

Examples of imminent health hazards within a food establishment include:
- Foodborne Illness Outbreak
- Water main break
- Power Outage
- Back up of Sewage
- Pest Infestation
- Loss of Refrigeration

The Person in Charge (PIC)/manager should **call the State and Local Regulatory Authority** if one of these events occurs.

If an imminent health hazard occurs, the State and Local Regulatory Authority may require:
- Immediate corrective action to take place
  - Corrective action includes:
    - Requiring employees to stop performing improper procedures immediately, and instructing them on how to do things the correct way
    - Retraining employees who repeatedly perform tasks incorrectly
- Immediate shutdown of the operation until the establishment can prove there is no longer a threat/emergency

REVIEW QUESTIONS

Food Safety Temperature Review

Directions: Read each question below and choose the correct answer for each question.

1. The Extreme Danger Zone or the area that promotes the most bacteria growth is   *
   _____.

   Mark only one oval.

   ◯ 41ºF to 135ºF

   ◯ 70ºF to 125ºF

   ◯ 70ºF to 135ºF

   ◯ 41ºF to 125ºF

2. What is the minimum internal temperature that hot foods must be held at to prevent *
   the growth of bacteria and other pathogens?

   Mark only one oval.

   ◯ 115°F

   ◯ 145°F

   ◯ 135°F

   ◯ 125°F

3. Cut tomatoes should be stored at what minimum internal temperature? *

   Mark only one oval.

   ◯ 45°F

   ◯ 51°F

   ◯ 55°F

   ◯ 41°F

4. What is the correct temperature to display deli meat? *

   Mark only one oval.

   ○ 45ºF

   ○ 70ºF

   ○ 135ºF

   ○ 41ºF

5. Food left in the temperature danger zone for more than _____ hours should be *
   thrown away.

   Mark only one oval.

   ○ 2

   ○ 4

   ○ 6

   ○ 8

6. Baked spaghetti was taken out of the oven at 10:30 am and placed on a buffet that *
   does not have temperature control. What time must the spaghetti be served by or
   thrown out?

   Mark only one oval.

   ○ 11:30 am

   ○ 1:30 pm

   ○ 2:30 pm

   ○ 3: 30 pm

7. What temperature must cooked green beans reach to be safely hot-held for service? *

Mark only one oval.

○ 145°F

○ 155°F

○ 135°F

○ 165°F

8. What is the temperature danger zone? *

Mark only one oval.

○ 70ºF to 125ºF

○ 41ºF to 135ºF

○ 70ºF to 135ºF

○ 41ºF to 125ºF

9. How often should you check the holding temperature of food to leave time for corrective action? *

Mark only one oval.

○ Every 4 hours

○ Every 6 hours

○ Every 2 hours

○ Every 8 hours

10. What should a food handler do with a carton of eggs that is delivered at 49°F? *

Mark only one oval.

◯ Quickly refrigerate the carton

◯ Reject the carton

◯ Freeze the carton until ready for use

◯ Only use the eggs for cooked dishes

Temperature/Time Controlled for Safety Review

Directions: Read each question below and choose the correct answer for each question.

1. Which food is not a TCS protein? *

   Mark only one oval.

   ◯ Uncooked garbanzo beans

   ◯ Raw pork chop

   ◯ Raw shrimp

   ◯ Raw salmon

2. How long can cooked bacon sit out as long as there is no moisture? *

   Mark only one oval.

   ◯ 12 days

   ◯ 2 days

   ◯ 7 days

   ◯ 4 days

3. Which food is a TCS food? *

   Mark only one oval.

   ◯ Whole uncut melons

   ◯ Bananas

   ◯ Uncooked rice

   ◯ Sprouts

4. What seafood dish not made with heat uses lime juice to kill the pathogens in the food? *

Mark only one oval.

○ Ceviche

○ Eggs Benedict

○ Seafood Pasta

○ Shrimp Boil

5. What does the acronym FAT TOM stand for? *

Mark only one oval.

○ Food, Acidity, Taste, Texture, Oxygen, Moisture

○ Flavor, Aroma, Taste, Texture, Oxygen, Moisture

○ Flavor, Acidity, Temperature, Taste, Oxygen, Moisture

○ Food, Acidity, Temperature, Time, Oxygen, Moisture

6. Which food is a TCS food? *

Mark only one oval.

○ Uncooked Pinto Beans

○ Cooked Brown Rice

○ Uncooked White Rice

○ Uncooked Linguine Noodles

7. Which juice is commonly used in cooking to control pathogens? *

   Mark only one oval.

   ( ) Apple juice

   ( ) Orange juice

   ( ) Lemon/lime juice

   ( ) Grape juice

8. Which food is a TCS food? *

   Mark only one oval.

   ( ) Olive oil infused with garlic and herbs

   ( ) Plain olive oil

   ( ) Whole uncut tomato

   ( ) Uncooked elbow macaroni noodles

9. Which is an example of a mechanically altered or messed with meat? *

   Mark only one oval.

   ( ) Raw ground turkey or raw ground beef

   ( ) Raw shrimp

   ( ) Raw steak

   ( ) Raw flounder

10. Which one of these is NOT a TCS food? *

Mark only one oval.

- ◯ Milk
- ◯ Coffee
- ◯ Cheese
- ◯ Eggs

Types of Contamination Review

Directions: Read each question below and choose the correct answer for each question.

1. What is the purpose of Material Data Safety Sheets? *

   Mark only one oval.

   - ( ) Informs customers about the types of TCS foods served in the operation
   - ( ) Keeps a running inventory of chemicals used in the operation
   - ( ) Informs staff of safe use and hazards of chemical used in the operation
   - ( ) Provides information on non food-grade equipment used in the operation

2. Cooking or freezing will always destroy toxins. *

   Mark only one oval.

   - ( ) True
   - ( ) False

3. What is the best way to prevent foodborne illness? *

   Mark only one oval.

   - ( ) Handwashing
   - ( ) Training employees on kitchen hazards
   - ( ) Monitoring employee activity at all times
   - ( ) Training customers on how to properly order foods so that they can avoid foods that could make them sick

4. Which of these is a biological contaminant? *

Mark only one oval.

◯ Ammonia Cleaning Solution

◯ Band-Aid

◯ Hair

◯ Bacteria

5. Which of these is a physical contaminant? *

Mark only one oval.

◯ Pathogens

◯ Bleach Cleaning Solution

◯ Parasites

◯ Hair and Hair accessories

6. The FDA A.L.E.R.T was designed to prevent what type of contamination? *

Mark only one oval.

◯ Biological

◯ Intentional/Deliberate

◯ Physical

◯ Chemical

7. What does the A in A.L.E.R.T stand for? *

Mark only one oval.

- ⬭ Assure
- ⬭ Accept
- ⬭ Aroma
- ⬭ Associates

8. What does the L in A.L.E.R.T stand for? *

Mark only one oval.

- ⬭ Locate
- ⬭ List
- ⬭ Look
- ⬭ Limit

9. What does the E in A.L.E.R.T stand for? *

Mark only one oval.

- ⬭ Evaporate
- ⬭ Edit
- ⬭ Employees
- ⬭ Exposed

10. What does the R in A.L.E.R.T stand for? *

Mark only one oval.

⬭ Repeat

⬭ Reports

⬭ Revise

⬭ Reduce

11. What does the T in A.L.E.R.T stand for? *

Mark only one oval.

⬭ Threat

⬭ Temperature

⬭ Time

⬭ Taste

Cleaning & Sanitizing Review

Directions: Read each question below and choose the correct answer for each question.

1. How often should you clean and sanitize for continual use? *

   Mark only one oval.

   ⬭ Every 2 hours

   ⬭ Every 4 hours

   ⬭ Every 8 hours

   ⬭ Every 24 hours

2. Butcher equipment/meat cutter in a refrigerated environment must be cleaned and *
   sanitized every _____.

   Mark only one oval.

   ⬭ Every 2 hours

   ⬭ Every 4 hours

   ⬭ Every 24 hours

   ⬭ Every 8 hours

3. What must be cleaned and sanitized as opposed to just being cleaned? *

   Mark only one oval.

   ⬭ Food Contact Surfaces

   ⬭ Floors

   ⬭ Walls

   ⬭ Outdoor garbage containers

4. What Standard Operating Procedure (SOP) determines the who, what, and when *
of cleaning the facility?

Mark only one oval.

- ◯ Kitchen Maintenance Schedule
- ◯ Master Cleaning Schedule
- ◯ Facility Maintenance Schedule
- ◯ Staff Cleaning List

5. What should a food handler do before starting the 5-step process for cleaning & *
sanitizing?

Mark only one oval.

- ◯ Measure the concentration of the cleaning solution
- ◯ Remove food from the counter area
- ◯ Apply hand sanitizer to their hands
- ◯ Wash, rinse, and sanitize the three-compartment sink

6. What is the correct order of the 5-step process for cleaning & sanitizing? *

Mark only one oval.

- ◯ Wash, scrape or remove food, sanitize, rinse, air-dry
- ◯ Scrape or remove food, wash, rinse, sanitize, air-dry
- ◯ Rinse, wash, sanitize, scrape or remove food, air-dry
- ◯ Wash, scrape or remove food, rinse, sanitize, air-dry

7. A food handler can _____ with chemicals or hot water/heat to reduce pathogens to * safe levels.

Mark only one oval.

- ◯ Sanitize
- ◯ Clean
- ◯ Rinse
- ◯ Air-Dry

8. Which is not an approved chemical for sanitizing? *

Mark only one oval.

- ◯ Iodine
- ◯ Quats
- ◯ Chlorine/Bleach
- ◯ All of these are approved chemicals for sanitizing
- ◯ None of these are approved chemicals for sanitizing

9. What should the temperature of the water be in the three-compartment sink? *

Mark only one oval.

- ◯ At least 110°F
- ◯ At least 130°F
- ◯ At least 171°F
- ◯ At least 180°F

10. What should a food handler do to test the concentration of sanitizer in water? *

Mark only one oval.

◯ Visually inspect the color of the water after adding the chemical to it

◯ Use a thermometer to measure the temperature of the water

◯ Make an educated guess about how much chemical they put into the water

◯ Use test strips to measure the concentration of chemical in the water

Cleaning & Sanitizing Review (2)

Directions: Read each question below and choose the correct answer for each question.

1. Which two chemicals have a contact time of at least 30 seconds? *

   Mark only one oval.

   ⬭ Chlorine and Iodine

   ⬭ Chlorine and Quats

   ⬭ Iodine and Quats

2. Which chemical has a contact time of at least 7 seconds? *

   Mark only one oval.

   ⬭ Iodine

   ⬭ Quats

   ⬭ Chlorine/Bleach

3. What does ppm stand for? *

   Mark only one oval.

   ⬭ parts per million

   ⬭ parts per measurement

   ⬭ parts per milliliters

   ⬭ parts per millimeters

4. What is the ppm for Chlorine/Bleach? *

Mark only one oval.

◯ 12.5-25 ppm

◯ 50-99 ppm

◯ Differs based on Manufacture Recommendations

5. What is the ppm for Iodine? *

Mark only one oval.

◯ 50-99 ppm

◯ Differs based on Manufacturer Recommendations

◯ 12.5-25 ppm

6. What is the ppm for Quats? *

Mark only one oval.

◯ 50-99 ppm

◯ 12.5-25 ppm

◯ Differs based on Manufacture Recommendations

7. Which one of these is not one of the five factors that influence the effectiveness of * sanitizer?

Mark only one oval.

◯ Concentration

◯ Temperature

◯ Contact time

◯ Water Color

◯ Water Hardness

◯ pH

8. Which statement is NOT true about cleaning products? *

Mark only one oval.

◯ Cleaning products should be stable.

◯ Cleaning products should be safe to use.

◯ Cleaning products should be non-corrosive.

◯ All of these statements are true about cleaning products.

◯ None of these statements are true about cleaning products.

9. Employees should have access to cleaning products at all times. *

Mark only one oval.

◯ True

◯ False

10. What temperature should the water be in the three-compartment sink when the *
    food handler is sanitizing with hot water?

    Mark only one oval.

    ◯ 171°F

    ◯ 110°F

    ◯ 180°F

    ◯ 145°F

11. What temperature should the water be in a dishwasher/sanitizing machine? *

    Mark only one oval.

    ◯ 171°F

    ◯ 180°F

    ◯ 110°F

    ◯ 145°F

12. It is recommended that you use a cloth to dry dishes to prevent the spread of *
    bacteria.

    Mark only one oval.

    ◯ True

    ◯ False

13. What is the correct order of the three-compartment sink? *

Mark only one oval.

- ◯ Detergent and hot water, sanitizer, clean water
- ◯ Sanitizer, clean water, detergent and hot water
- ◯ Clean water, detergent and hot water, sanitizer
- ◯ Detergent and hot water, clean water, sanitizer

Cleaning & Sanitizing Review (3)

Directions: Read each question below and choose the correct answer for each question.

1. What is another name for a mop sink? *

   Mark only one oval.

   - ◯ Linen Sink
   - ◯ Cleaning Sink
   - ◯ Sanitizing Sink
   - ◯ Service Sink

2. Where should dirty linens be placed? *

   Mark only one oval.

   - ◯ On the floor by the washing machine
   - ◯ In any sink away from food prep areas
   - ◯ In a service sink
   - ◯ In a dirty linen bag

3. Where should sanitizer buckets be placed? *

   Mark only one oval.

   - ◯ Below work tables and at least 4 inches off the floor
   - ◯ Below work tables and at least 6 inches off the floor
   - ◯ On the food prep table, but at least 6 inches away from food
   - ◯ On the shelf above food, but at least 6 inches above the food

4. How often should should sanitizing solution in buckets be changed? *

Mark only one oval.

- ⃝ Every 4 hours
- ⃝ Every 24 hours
- ⃝ Every 12 hours
- ⃝ Every 8 hours

5. How should mops and brooms be stored when not in use? *

Mark only one oval.

- ⃝ Hanging on a hook
- ⃝ On the floor in the corner
- ⃝ In a bucket without water
- ⃝ In the mop sink

Purchasing & Receiving Food Review

Directions: Read each question below and choose the correct answer for each question.

1. Food suppliers should be _____. *

   Mark only one oval.

   - ( ) Recommended and Reliable
   - ( ) Affordable and Close in Proximity
   - ( ) Approved and Reputable
   - ( ) Recommended and Close in Proximity

2. What type of thermometer is used for checking the temperature inside a cooler or oven? *

   Mark only one oval.

   - ( ) Air probe
   - ( ) Surface probe
   - ( ) Immersion probe
   - ( ) Penetration probe

3. What do you call a delivery in which the supplier is given a key to the establishment, the delivery occurs after hours, and the supplier is responsible for putting the product in its proper storage location? *

Mark only one oval.

◯ Supplier-assisted delivery

◯ No recipient delivery

◯ Key drop delivery

◯ Delayed recipient delivery

4. What type of thermometer is used for checking the temperature of flat cooking equipment like a griddle? *

Mark only one oval.

◯ Surface probe

◯ Immersion probe

◯ Penetration probe

◯ Air probe

5. When should a food handler or kitchen manager inspect a food supply delivery? *

Mark only one oval.

◯ Within 4 hours of receiving the delivery

◯ Immediately

◯ At the end of the day when the operation closes

◯ Within 24 hours of receiving the delivery

6. Thermometers need to be +/- how many degrees to be accurate? *

Mark only one oval.

- ◯ 4
- ◯ 10
- ◯ 6
- ◯ 2

7. What is the best way to calibrate a thermometer? *

Mark only one oval.

- ◯ Hot water calibration
- ◯ Cold/ice water calibration
- ◯ Warm water calibration
- ◯ Room temperature water calibration

8. When should thermometers be cleaned and sanitized? *

Mark only one oval.

- ◯ Before each use
- ◯ After each use
- ◯ Before and after each use
- ◯ Only when checking the temperature of different food items

9. What type of thermometer is used for checking the temperature of liquids? *

Mark only one oval.

◯ Surface probe

◯ Penetration probe

◯ Air probe

◯ Immersion probe

10. What type of thermometer is used for checking the internal temperature of foods *
    like hamburger patties?

Mark only one oval.

◯ Penetration probe

◯ Immersion probe

◯ Surface probe

◯ Air probe

11. Which type of instrument changes colors when it recognizes time-temperature *
    abuse?

Mark only one oval.

◯ Penetration probe

◯ Time-Temperature Indicator (TTI)

◯ Surface probe

◯ Air probe

Purchasing & Receiving Food Review (2)

Directions: Read each question below and choose the correct answer for each question.

1. Game animals such as deer _____. *

    Mark only one oval.

    ◯ can only be hunted in wild areas no more than 50 miles from the establishment

    ◯ must be commercially raised for food

    ◯ can only be hunted in wild areas approved by the kitchen manager

    ◯ must come from one of the five states listed on the USDA Game Hunting List

2. What should you NOT do to food items linked to a foodborne illness outbreak? *

    Mark only one oval.

    ◯ Remove from inventory

    ◯ Separate from other food items

    ◯ Label "Do not discard and do not use"

    ◯ Store food items in the refrigerator

3. Food donations are acceptable when: *

    Mark only one oval.

    ◯ Food was held, prepared, and packaged according to requirements of the restaurant chain

    ◯ Food was held, prepared, and packaged according to requirements of the restaurant owner

    ◯ Food was held, prepared, and packaged according to requirements of the local government

    ◯ Food was held, prepared and packaged according to the Food Code

84

4. Where should you place cooler thermometers for testing the temperature? *

Mark only one oval.

⬭ In the warmest part of the cooler

⬭ In the coolest part of the cooler

⬭ In the darkest part of the cooler

⬭ In the brightest part of the cooler

5. Eggs, shellstock, and milk can be received up to a temperature of _____. *

Mark only one oval.

⬭ 45°F

⬭ 55°F

⬭ 65°F

⬭ 75°F

6. How long should shellstock indentification tags be kept? *

Mark only one oval.

⬭ 90 days from receipt of the delivery

⬭ 90 days from the day the last item has been sold or served from the bag

⬭ 30 days from the day the last item has been sold or served from the bag

⬭ 30 days from receipt of the delivery

7. Where should you place oven thermometers for testing temperature? *

Mark only one oval.

- In the warmest part of the oven
- In the darkest part of the oven
- In the brightest part of the oven
- In the coolest part of the oven

8. How long is the incubation period for Hepatitis A? *

Mark only one oval.

- 30 days
- 45 days
- 60 days
- 90 days

9. Why must fish packaged using Reduced Oxygen Packaging (ROP) be frozen until *
used?

Mark only one oval.

- To help control parasites
- To help maintain flavor
- To help maintain texture
- To help control odor

10. Mushrooms used in food prep _____. *

Mark only one oval.

◯ can come from wild areas within 25 miles of the food service establishment

◯ must come from approved foragers to control toxins

◯ can come from wild areas within 50 miles of the food service establishment

◯ must come from one of the five states listed on the USDA Foragers List

11. Where should you place an ambient hanging thermometer? *

Mark only one oval.

◯ In the warmest part of a walk-in storage cooler

◯ In the coolest part of a walk-in storage cooler

◯ In the darkest part of a walk-in storage cooler

◯ In the brightest part of a walk-in storage cooler

Minimum Internal Cooking Temperature Review

Directions: Read each question below and choose the correct answer for each question.

1. What is the purpose of a consumer advisory on a menu? *

   Mark only one oval.

   ⬭ To warn customers about the health risks of eating red meat

   ⬭ To advise customers on how different cooking methods can alter the flavor of foods

   ⬭ To warn customers about the risks of eating raw and undercooked foods

   ⬭ To warn customers about the health risks of eating more than 2,000 calories per day

2. A restaurant wants to use packaged/frozen corn or peas on their salad bar. In order *
   to cut down on the risk of foodborne illness, what must the restaurant do prior to
   placing these items on the salad bar?

   Mark only one oval.

   ⬭ Thaw and wash the items

   ⬭ Thaw them only

   ⬭ Wash them only

   ⬭ Cook them items according to the instructions on the package

3. What is the minimum internal cooking temperature for anything reheated or anything that is microwaved? *

Mark only one oval.

○ 135°F

○ 145°F

○ 155°F

○ 165°F

4. What is the minimum internal cooking temperature for RTE foods? *

Mark only one oval.

○ 135°F held for a minimum of 15 seconds

○ 145°F held for a minimum of 15 seconds

○ 155°F held for a minimum of 17 seconds

○ 165°F (1 second, instantaneous)

5. What is the minimum internal cooking temperature for whole meat, chops, filets, and steaks? *

Mark only one oval.

○ 135°F held for a minimum of 15 seconds

○ 145°F held for a minimum of 15 seconds

○ 155°F held for a minimum of 17 seconds

○ 165°F (1 second, instantaneous)

6. What is the minimum internal cooking temperature for seafood? *

Mark only one oval.

◯ 135°F held for a minimum of 15 seconds

◯ 145°F held for a minimum of 15 seconds

◯ 155°F held for a minimum of 17 seconds

◯ 165°F (1 second, instantaneous)

7. What is the minimum internal cooking temperature for ground meat/messed with   *
meat?

Mark only one oval.

◯ 135°F held for a minimum of 15 seconds

◯ 145°F held for a minimum of 15 seconds

◯ 155°F held for a minimum of 17 seconds

◯ 165°F (1 second, instantaneous)

8. What is the minimum internal cooking temperature for buffet eggs or mechanically   *
tenderized meat?

Mark only one oval.

◯ 135°F

◯ 145°F

◯ 155°F

◯ 165°F

9. What is the minimum internal cooking temperature for ground, chopped, or minced *
   seafood?

   Mark only one oval.

   ◯ 135°F

   ◯ 145°F

   ◯ 155°F

   ◯ 165°F

10. What is the minimum internal cooking temperature for anything stuffed or anything *
    with two or more ingredients like a stew?

    Mark only one oval.

    ◯ 135°F

    ◯ 145°F

    ◯ 155°F

    ◯ 165°F

11. What is the minimum internal cooking temperature for over medium eggs? *

    Mark only one oval.

    ◯ 135°F

    ◯ 145°F

    ◯ 155°F

    ◯ 165°F

12. What is the minimum internal cooking temperature for vacuum-tumbled meats *
    with marinade?

    Mark only one oval.

    ○ 135°F

    ○ 145°F

    ○ 155°F

    ○ 165°F

13. When parcooking food, food should not be cooked longer than _____ minutes? *

    Mark only one oval.

    ○ 30

    ○ 45

    ○ 60

    ○ 90

14. After parcooking food, food should be held in the refrigerator at _____ or lower and *
    away from RTE food.

    Mark only one oval.

    ○ 135°F

    ○ 125°F

    ○ 41°F

    ○ 70°F

15. Restaurants need approval from the State and Local Regulatory Authority prior to *
parcooking food.

Mark only one oval.

⚪ True

⚪ False

16. When parcooking food, food must be _____ prior to serving. *

Mark only one oval.

⚪ Completely thawed out

⚪ Left on the storage shelf at room temperature

⚪ Cooked no longer than 30 minutes

⚪ Cooked to the correct minimum internal cooking temperature

Cooling Food Review

Directions: Read each question below and choose the correct answer for each question.

1. When cooling food, the food temperature must go from 135°F to 70°F within the   *
    first _____.

    Mark only one oval.

    ◯ 1 hour

    ◯ 2 hours

    ◯ 4 hours

    ◯ 6 hours

2. When cooling food, the food temperature must go from 70°F to 41°F within the   *
    remaining _____.

    Mark only one oval.

    ◯ 1 hour

    ◯ 2 hours

    ◯ 4 hours

    ◯ 6 hours

3. How long should the total cooling process take? *

    Mark only one oval.

    ◯ 1 hour

    ◯ 2 hours

    ◯ 4 hours

    ◯ 6 hours

4. What should the operation have to demonstrate that food has been properly cooled? *

Mark only one oval.

⬭ A kitchen manager that can keep a record in their head of how long food has been cooling

⬭ A cooldown log

⬭ Any staff member that can keep a record in their head of how long food has been cooling

⬭ A designated food handler that can keep a record in their head of how long food has been cooling

5. Which one of these is NOT a good way to cool food down? *

Mark only one oval.

⬭ Larger portions

⬭ Ice as an ingredient or ice paddle

⬭ Ice water bath

⬭ Blast chiller

6. Which statement is NOT true about "Cook Chill" food? *　　　　0 points

Mark only one oval.

⬭ Food must be consumed within 7 days, but no more than 30 days from date of packaging

⬭ Food may be frozen with no time limit on the shelf life

⬭ Food is stored in Reduced Oxygen Packaging (ROP)

⬭ Food must be cooled to 34°F within 7 days of reaching 41°F

95

Facility Requirements Review

Directions: Read each question below and choose the correct answer for each question.

1. Floor coving is designed to _____. *

   Mark only one oval.

   ⬭ prevent floods

   ⬭ provide better lighting in the kitchen

   ⬭ prevent backflow

   ⬭ reduce sharpness between the floor and wall and make the floor easier to sweep

2. Floors, walls, and ceilings should be _____. *

   Mark only one oval.

   ⬭ leakproof, waterproof, and easy to clean

   ⬭ smooth, durable, and easy to clean

   ⬭ porous and able to absorb water/spills

   ⬭ painted white or a neutral color to not be distracting to food handlers

3. All kitchen lighting should _____. *

   Mark only one oval.

   ⬭ be at least 4 feet of the floor

   ⬭ have a protective shield or protective lens

   ⬭ only contain energy efficient bulbs

   ⬭ be approved by the state and local regulatory authority

4. What is required to prevent the buildup of grease and moisture in the kitchen? *

Mark only one oval.

- ( ) Hoods and proper ventilation system
- ( ) Floor fans
- ( ) Restaurant grade cleaning solutions
- ( ) Non-slip flooring and countertops

5. What do you call the physical link between a safe & unsafe water source? *

Mark only one oval.

- ( ) Cross-contamination
- ( ) Cross-contact
- ( ) Cross-reversion
- ( ) Cross-connection

6. Backflow or backsiphonage occurs when _____. *

Mark only one oval.

- ( ) TCS liquids leak in the refrigerator
- ( ) chemicals used for sanitizing burn holes in the pipes of the plumbing system
- ( ) water flows in reverse due to a change in pressure within the plumbing system
- ( ) there is an air gap

7. What is the only guaranteed way to prevent backflow? *

Mark only one oval.

◯ Vacuum breaker

◯ Air gap

◯ Cross-connection

◯ Larger pipes

8. Which statement is TRUE about vacuum breakers? *

Mark only one oval.

◯ They allow water to flow in both directions

◯ They allow water to flow in one direction

◯ They allow for easy cleanup of dirt and debris on the floor

◯ They allow for easy cleanup of dirt and debris in sink areas

9. All of the following are ways to describe water that can be used for food preparation *
EXCEPT:

Mark only one oval.

◯ Prepared & Unprepared

◯ Safe & Unsafe

◯ Potable & Non-Potable

◯ Drinkable & Undrinkable

10. What is required if you put a hose at the end of a faucet? *

Mark only one oval.

○ A bucket with a 14" or larger diameter

○ Vacuum breaker

○ A bucket with height of at least 14"

○ A bucket placed over a floor drain in case of overflow

11. Kitchen equipment must be approved by: *

Mark only one oval.

○ USDA

○ FDA

○ NSF, ANSI, or ANAB

○ State and Local Regulatory Authority

12. All of the following marks demonstrate certification of sanitation EXCEPT: *

Mark only one oval.

○ CDC Certification mark

○ NSF mark

○ UL EPH mark

○ ETL Sanitation mark

Facility Requirements Review (2)

Directions: Read each question below and choose the correct answer for each question.

1. Floor equipment must be _____ off the floor. *

   Mark only one oval.

   ◯ 4 inches

   ◯ 6 inches

   ◯ 8 inches

   ◯ 12 inches

2. Counter equipment must be _____ off the countertop. *

   Mark only one oval.

   ◯ 4 inches

   ◯ 6 inches

   ◯ 8 inches

   ◯ 12 inches

3. Floor equipment must be on _____ for easy movement for cleaning. *

   Mark only one oval.

   ◯ a non-slip equipment pad

   ◯ a plastic equipment pad

   ◯ casters/wheels

   ◯ a rubber equipment pad

4. Indoor garbage cans must _____. *

Mark only one oval.

- ( ) be leakproof, waterproof, and easy to clean
- ( ) be smooth, durable, and easy to clean
- ( ) have tight fitting lids
- ( ) be sitting on a concrete/asphalt slab in the kitchen

5. Outdoor garbage cans must _____. *

Mark only one oval.

- ( ) be leakproof, waterproof, and easy to clean
- ( ) have tight fitting lids and be sitting on concrete/asphalt
- ( ) be smooth, durable, and easy to clean
- ( ) be at least 6 inches off the ground

6. When talking about pest control, harborage is another word for _____. *

Mark only one oval.

- ( ) shelter
- ( ) food
- ( ) water
- ( ) quantity

101

7. Which is not a way to control pests? *

Mark only one oval.

○ Installing an air gap

○ Installing an air curtain

○ Inspecting all food shipments immediately

○ Installing screens and sealing outside openings

8. Who should the PIC contact if they see signs of a pest infestastion? *

Mark only one oval.

○ Licensed Pest Control Operator

○ Front of the House Staff

○ Back of the House Staff

○ FDA

9. Floor equipment not on casters/wheels must _____. *

Mark only one oval.

○ be on a non-slip equipment pad

○ weigh less than 100 lbs.

○ weigh less than 50 lbs.

○ be mounted to the floor

10. All of the following are things that you should deny pests in order to control them *
EXCEPT:

Mark only one oval.

◯ Food

◯ Water

◯ Shelter

◯ All of these are things that you should deny pests

◯ None of these are things that you should deny pests

SHENS Review

Directions: Read each question below and choose the correct answer for each question.

1. Which type of Hepatitis is the only type that is a foodborne illness? *

   Mark only one oval.

   ◯ Hepatitis A

   ◯ Hepatitis B

   ◯ Hepatitis C

2. Which SHENS condition is caused by raw and undercooked poultry and eggs? *

   Mark only one oval.

   ◯ E. Coli

   ◯ Shigella

   ◯ Salmonella

   ◯ Norovirus

3. Which SHENS condition is caused by RTE foods contaminated with feces or bad   *
   shellfish?

   Mark only one oval.

   ◯ Norovirus

   ◯ Salmonella

   ◯ Shigella

   ◯ E. Coli

4. Which SHENS condition is caused by animal feces like cow intestines or meat contaminated during slaughtering? *

Mark only one oval.

◯ Salmonella

◯ E. Coli

◯ Shigella

◯ Norovirus

5. Which SHENS condition is caused by feces from food and water, or feces carried by flies? *

Mark only one oval.

◯ Shigella

◯ Salmonella

◯ Norovirus

◯ E. Coli

6. Jaundice is a symptom of which SHENS condition? *

Mark only one oval.

◯ Norovirus

◯ Shigella

◯ Salmonella

◯ Hepatitis A

7. What are the two types of salmonella? *

Mark only one oval.

⬭ Type A and Type B

⬭ Type 1 and Type 2

⬭ Regular and Typhi/Typhoid

⬭ SAL-1 and SAL-2

8. Hepatitis A is a disease of which organ? *

Mark only one oval.

⬭ Kidneys

⬭ Gallbladder

⬭ Heart

⬭ Liver

9. An excluded food handler cannot return to work until _____. *

Mark only one oval.

⬭ they have been symptom-free for at least 24 hours

⬭ they are feeling better and they are showing only 25% of symptoms

⬭ they have been symptom-free for at least 7 days and they have been cleared by a note from their doctor

⬭ they have been symptom-free for at least 24 hours and they have been cleared by a note from their doctor

10. Yellowing of the skin or eyes is a symptom of which condition? *

Mark only one oval.

- ( ) Hepatitis B
- ( ) Jaundice
- ( ) Shigella
- ( ) Salmonella

SHENS Review (2)

Directions: Read each question below and choose the correct answer for each question.

1. Food handlers that are restricted from the food operation _____. *

   Mark only one oval.

   ◯ can work in the operation, but they cannot work around food

   ◯ can work in the operation and resume normal duties including preparing food

   ◯ cannot come to work at all

   ◯ can work in the operation, but can only prepare food

2. Food handlers that are excluded from the food operation _____. *

   Mark only one oval.

   ◯ can work in the operation, but they cannot work around food

   ◯ can work in the operation and resume normal duties including preparing food

   ◯ cannot come to work at all

   ◯ can work in the operation, but can only perform duties that do not involve food

3. Which condition would cause a food handler to be excluded from the operation? *

   Mark only one oval.

   ◯ Sore throat

   ◯ Jaundice

   ◯ Fever

   ◯ Migraine Headache

4. Which condition would cause a food handler to be restricted from the operation? *

Mark only one oval.

○ Vomiting

○ Sore throat

○ Diarrhea

○ Jaundice

5. A food handler with a SHENS diagnosis, _____. *　　　　　　　　　　0 points

Mark only one oval.

○ must be restricted from the operation for 24 hours

○ must be restricted until they feel better

○ must be excluded from the operation for a minimum of 14 days

○ must be excluded from the operation until cleared by a note from their doctor

6. Regardless of the illness, a food handler that works in an establishment that serves　*
a group in the YOPI population _____.

Mark only one oval.

○ should not come to work at all

○ must be restricted from food preparation duties for 7 days

○ must be restricted from food preparation duties for 14 days

○ must contact their kitchen manager and get their opinion on whether or not they should come to work

7. What is the most common cause of a SHENS diagnosis? *

Mark only one oval.

- ◯ Failing to cook food correctly
- ◯ Purchasing food from unsafe sources
- ◯ Feces
- ◯ Holding food at incorrect temperatures

8. Restaurants must have written procedures for which two conditions? *

Mark only one oval.

- ◯ Headache and Vomiting
- ◯ Sore Throat and Fever
- ◯ Vomiting and Diarrhea
- ◯ Upset Stomach and Fever

9. What is the name of the agreement that states that a food handler must let the PIC *
know if they or someone in their household is diagnosed with a SHENS condition?

Mark only one oval.

- ◯ Employee Safety Agreement
- ◯ SHENS Prevention Agreement
- ◯ Employee Health Policy Agreement
- ◯ SHENS Employee Contract

10. Who should the PIC contact if someone is the establishment is diagnosed with a *
SHENS condition?

Mark only one oval.

◯ FDA

◯ State and Local Regulatory Authority

◯ CDC

◯ USDA

FAT TOM Review

Directions: Read each question below and choose the correct answer for each question.

1. What is the Temperature Danger Zone (TDZ)? *

   Mark only one oval.

   ◯ 70°F to 125°F

   ◯ 41°F to 135°F

   ◯ 70°F to 135°F

   ◯ 41°F to 70°F

2. What does the F in FAT TOM stand for? *

   Mark only one oval.

   ◯ Food

   ◯ Flavor

   ◯ Focus

   ◯ Facts

3. What does the A in FAT TOM stand for? *

   Mark only one oval.

   ◯ Aroma

   ◯ Assure

   ◯ Acidity

   ◯ Accept

4. There are two Ts in FAT TOM. What do they stand for? *

Mark only one oval.

- ◯ Taste and Texture
- ◯ Temperature and Texture
- ◯ Threat and Temperature
- ◯ Temperature and Time

5. What does the O in FAT TOM stand for? *

Mark only one oval.

- ◯ Omit
- ◯ Observe
- ◯ Optional
- ◯ Oxygen

6. What does the M in FAT TOM stand for? *

Mark only one oval.

- ◯ Moisture
- ◯ Maintain
- ◯ Measure
- ◯ Mix

7. Bacteria grow best in foods _____. *

Mark only one oval.

- with a high pH value
- with a low pH value (neutral to slightly acidic)
- that are highly alkaline
- with a pH value of 8-14

8. Bacteria grow well in foods with _____ levels of moisture. *

Mark only one oval.

- Low
- High
- Minimal
- Undetectable

9. Which range that falls within the Temperature Danger Zone will cause bacteria grow rapidly? *

Mark only one oval.

- 70°F to 125°F
- 40°F to 70°F
- 125°F to 135°F
- 41°F to 71°F

114

10. As the amount of time food spends in Temperature Danger Zone increases, *
_____.

Mark only one oval.

○ The opportunity for bacteria to grow to unsafe levels increases

○ The opportunity for bacteria to grow to unsafe levels decreases.

○ The opportunity for bacteria to grow to unsafe levels neither increases or decreases

○ There is no time limit for how long food should be allowed to remain in the Temperature Danger Zone

Foodborne Illness Review

Directions: Read each question below and choose the correct answer for each question.

1. Which is NOT a role of the USDA? *

   Mark only one oval.

   ⬭ Inspects meat, poultry, and eggs packaging

   ⬭ Inspects food shipped to suppliers

   ⬭ Issues the Food Code

   ⬭ Inspects food processing plants

2. Which is NOT a role of the FDA? *

   Mark only one oval.

   ⬭ Scientific Research

   ⬭ Issues the Food Code

   ⬭ Inspects food that crosses state lines

   ⬭ Inspects meat, poultry, and eggs packaging

3. Which agency handles cases of diseases and outbreaks? *

   Mark only one oval.

   ⬭ USDA

   ⬭ FDA

   ⬭ ANSI

   ⬭ CDC

116

4. Any illness from eating contaminated food is called a(n) _____. *

   Mark only one oval.

   ⬭ outbreak

   ⬭ foodborne illness

   ⬭ epidemic

   ⬭ occurrence

5. Two or more cases of people eating the same contaminated food is called a(n)   *
   _____.

   Mark only one oval.

   ⬭ outbreak

   ⬭ foodborne illness

   ⬭ case

   ⬭ occurrence

6. One risk factor for foodborne illness is purchasing food from _____. sources. *

   Mark only one oval.

   ⬭ unsafe

   ⬭ approved

   ⬭ reputable

   ⬭ reliable

7. States are required by law to adopt the Food Code. *

   Mark only one oval.

   ⬭ True

   ⬭ False

8. One risk factor for foodborne illness is failing to _____ food correctly. *

Mark only one oval.

○ cut

○ choose

○ cook

○ collect

9. One risk factor for foodborne illness is holding food at _____ temperatures. *

Mark only one oval.

○ correct

○ approved

○ incorrect

○ minimum internal

10. One risk factor for foodborne illness is using _____ equipment. *

Mark only one oval.

○ approved

○ contaminated

○ reliable

○ sanitized

11. One risk factor for foodborne illness is _____ personal hygiene. *

Mark only one oval.

○ minimal

○ poor

○ excellent

○ quality

12. Which statement is NOT true about time-temperature abuse? *

Mark only one oval.

○ It occurs when food is not being held at the right temperature for the right amount of time

○ It occurs when food is cooked to the right temperature, but it is cooked too long

○ It occurs when food is not being cooked at the right temperature for the right amount of time

○ It occurs when food is not being reheated to the right temperature for the right amount of time

Personal Hygiene Review

Directions: Read each question below and choose the correct answer for each question.

1. What are the five requirements for a handwashing station? *

   Mark only one oval.

   ◯ Hot & Cold Water, Soap, Single Use Paper Towel (or way to dry hands), Garbage Container, Nail Scrubber

   ◯ Hot & Cold Water, Hand Sanitizer, Single Use Paper Towel (or way to dry hands), Garbage Container, Signage

   ◯ Hot & Cold Water, Hand Sanitizer, Single Use Paper Towel (or way to dry hands), Garbage Container, Nail Scrubber

   ◯ Hot & Cold Water, Soap, Single Use Paper Towel (or way to dry hands), Garbage Container, Signage

2. The entire handwashing process should take approximately: *

   Mark only one oval.

   ◯ 10-15 seconds

   ◯ 20 seconds

   ◯ 10 seconds

   ◯ 12 seconds

3. How long should the food handler scrub their hands and arms when washing their hands? *

Mark only one oval.

- ⬭ 5 seconds
- ⬭ 10-15 seconds
- ⬭ 8 seconds
- ⬭ 5-10 seconds

4. What should the temperature of the water be in the handwashing sink? *

Mark only one oval.

- ⬭ 70°F
- ⬭ 85°F
- ⬭ 41°F
- ⬭ 135°F

5. What do you call a person that carries infections, but does not have any symptoms? *

Mark only one oval.

- ⬭ Carrier
- ⬭ Infector
- ⬭ Spreader
- ⬭ Passer

6. Hand sanitizers must be approved by which agency? *

Mark only one oval.

◯ FDA

◯ CDC

◯ USDA

◯ State and Local Regulatory Authority

7. Hand sanitizers should be at least _____ alcohol. *

Mark only one oval.

◯ 41%

◯ 60%

◯ 75%

◯ 91%

8. What must be worn on a finger with a cut on it? *

Mark only one oval.

◯ Nothing as long as the food handler properly washes their hands

◯ Band-Aid only

◯ Gauze wrapping

◯ Band-Aid and Glove/Finger Cot

9. What is the only acceptable piece of jewelry in the kitchen? *

Mark only one oval.

○ Watch

○ Medical Bracelet

○ Smooth plain band ring

○ Small stud earrings

10. What should you do before putting on gloves after doing things like switching   *
tasks, smoking/vaping, using the restroom, or taking out trash?

Mark only one oval.

○ Use hand sanitizer

○ Wash your hands

○ Use hand sanitizer and then put gloves on

○ Put gloves on without washing hands or using hand sanitizer

11. When is it acceptable to use hand sanitizer? *

Mark only one oval.

○ Only after washing your hands

○ Instead of washing your hands

○ When switching tasks

○ After using the restroom

Personal Hygiene Review (2)

Directions: Read each question below and choose the correct answer for each question.

1. A Band-Aid and glove, or a Band-Aid and finger cot are required if you have a cut on your finger. *

   Mark only one oval.

   ⬭ True

   ⬭ False

2. When are gloves NOT required? *

   Mark only one oval.

   ⬭ When washing produce or when handling foods that will be properly cooked

   ⬭ When handling RTE foods

   ⬭ When handling a freshly baked pizza

   ⬭ When handling unpackaged chips and cookies

3. A food handler should wear a beard guard if their beard is longer than _____. *

   Mark only one oval.

   ⬭ 1/8 inch

   ⬭ 1/2 inch

   ⬭ 1 inch

   ⬭ 1/4 inch

4. Which is an example of appropriate attire for a food handler? *

Mark only one oval.

○ Open-toed shoes

○ Reusable gloves

○ Shows with slippery bottoms

○ Clean apron and hat/hair net

5. What should food handlers do before using the bathroom? *

Mark only one oval.

○ Wash their hands

○ Change their gloves

○ Take off their aprons

○ Use hand sanitizer

6. A food handler's beverage: *

Mark only one oval.

○ should have a lid or straw, a label with their name on it, and be stored above food prep areas

○ should have a lid and a straw, a label with their name on it, and be stored away from food prep areas

○ does not have to have a lid or a straw as long as their name is on the container.

○ does not have to have a lid or a straw as long as their name is on the container and it is stored above food prep areas.

7. Where can food handlers smoke in a food service establishment? *

Mark only one oval.

◯ In the kitchen, but away from food prep areas

◯ Outside and away from food prep areas

◯ Food handlers should not smoke inside or outside the food service establishment

◯ In the kitchen, but a minimum of 6 feet away from food prep areas

8. It is okay to save gloves for later or for reuse in order to save money for the establishment. *

Mark only one oval.

◯ True

◯ False

9. Which item could potentially be a physical contaminant? *

Mark only one oval.

◯ Nail polish

◯ Clorox

◯ Iodine

◯ Quats

10. Why are gloves not required when dressing pizza? *

Mark only one oval.

- ◯ Because cooked pizza carries a low risk of contamination
- ◯ Because cooked pizza is not a TCS food
- ◯ Because cold pizza toppings are not TCS foods
- ◯ Because most pizza ovens reach a temperature of at least 450°F and pathogens will be killed at this temperature

11. Which is an acceptable action for a food handler? *

Mark only one oval.

- ◯ Drinking from an open container in the kitchen
- ◯ Chewing gum in the in kitchen
- ◯ Smoking outside the building at the food service establishment
- ◯ Eating from an open container in the kitchen

12. Which item could potentially be a physical contaminant? *

Mark only one oval.

- ◯ False eyelashes
- ◯ Bleach
- ◯ Dish detergent
- ◯ Bacteria

13. What should a food handler do after taking gloves off? *

Mark only one oval.

- ◯ Use hand sanitizer
- ◯ Nothing as long as they are not leaving the kitchen/food prep area
- ◯ Wash their hands
- ◯ Immediately put on a new set of gloves

14. Wounds and boils should be covered with a _____. *

Mark only one oval.

- ◯ Durable tight-fitting dressing only
- ◯ Loose fitting dressing and a glove
- ◯ Glove only
- ◯ Waterproof/impermeable dressing that is durable and tight-fitting, and a glove

Preparing Food Review

Directions: Read each question below and choose the correct answer for each question.

1. Which color cutting board should be used for dairy products? *

   Mark only one oval.

   ◯ White

   ◯ Yellow

   ◯ Blue

   ◯ Red

2. _____ is the transfer of harmful bacteria from one food to another. *

   Mark only one oval.

   ◯ Cross-connection

   ◯ Cross-contamination

   ◯ Cross-contact

   ◯ Cross-reversion

3. What should you do with equipment in between preparing different types of foods? *

   Mark only one oval.

   ◯ Rinse equipment thoroughly

   ◯ Wash, rinse, and sanitize equipment

   ◯ Rinse equipment in water that is at least 70°F

   ◯ Clean equipment

4. How should meals be prepared to prevent cross-contamination? *

Mark only one oval.

○ In any order

○ Poultry should be prepared first and RTE foods should be prepared last

○ In the order that the items go in the refrigerator

○ All like meats should be prepared first and all like vegetables should be prepared last

5. Which color cutting board should be used for raw seafood? *

Mark only one oval.

○ Yellow

○ Blue

○ Green

○ Purple

6. Which color cutting board should be used for raw pork/meat? *

Mark only one oval.

○ Yellow

○ Green

○ Brown

○ Red

7. Which color cutting board should be used for produce? *

   Mark only one oval.

   ◯ Green

   ◯ Yellow

   ◯ Blue

   ◯ Brown

8. Which color cutting board should be used for cooked food items? *

   Mark only one oval.

   ◯ Purple

   ◯ Brown

   ◯ Blue

   ◯ Red

9. Which color cutting board should be used for allergy foods? *

   Mark only one oval.

   ◯ Yellow

   ◯ Purple

   ◯ Blue

   ◯ White

Preparing & Storing Food Review

Directions: Read each question below and choose the correct answer for each question.

1. Which type of eggs should be used in eggs for Caesar salad dressing, homemade   *
   ranch dressing, and in nursing homes?

   Mark only one oval.

   ◯ White Eggs

   ◯ Brown Eggs

   ◯ Pasteurized Eggs

   ◯ Farm Fresh Eggs

2. When thawing food in water, the temperature of the water should not be higher   *
   than _____.

   Mark only one oval.

   ◯ 110°F

   ◯ 100°F

   ◯ 70°F

   ◯ 50°F

3. Which of these is NOT an approved way to thaw food? *

   Mark only one oval.

   ◯ On the countertop

   ◯ Microwave, but the food must be cooked immediately

   ◯ In the refrigerator

   ◯ As part of the cooking process

4. When storing food, dry goods should _____. *

Mark only one oval.

○ be stored on the floor next to recyclable products

○ have a label with a common name

○ be stored underneath the sink, but at least 4 inches away from chemicals

○ be stored on the counter, but at least 6 inches away from chemicals

5. Food can be kept for _____ in the refrigerator before having to be thrown away. *

Mark only one oval.

○ 7 days

○ 10 days

○ 14 days

○ 30 days

6. Ready-to-eat TCS foods like homemade ranch dressing must have a discard date if *
being held longer than _____.

Mark only one oval.

○ 7 days

○ 14 days

○ 24 hours

○ 3 days

133

7. Food that is held to be served on-site and is not in its original container must _____. *

   Mark only one oval.

   ○ have a label with a common name

   ○ have a label with discard date

   ○ be packaged with a label that shows the ingredients in descending order by weight.

   ○ have a label with a common name and a discard date

8. Prepared foods for retail sale, packaged foods, and Grab-N-Go items must _____. *

   Mark only one oval.

   ○ be held at a temperature no higher than 41°F

   ○ be held at a temperature no lower than 135°F

   ○ be in Reduced Oxygen Packaging (ROP)

   ○ be packaged with a label that shows the ingredients in descending order by weight

9. What is the FIFO method? *

   Mark only one oval.

   ○ Items with the earliest use-by/discard dates are stored behind items with later use-by/discard dates

   ○ Items with earliest use-by/discard dates are stored in front of items with later use-by/discard dates

   ○ Items with earliest use-by/discard dates are stored next to items with later use-by/discard dates

   ○ Items with earlies use-by/discard dates are stored on top of items with later use-by/discard dates

10. What is the formula for calculating the discard date of an item? *

Mark only one oval.

◯ Date Made + 7 days

◯ Date Made + 6 days

◯ Date Made + 12 days

◯ Date Made + 10 days

Food Allergies Review

Directions: Read each question below and choose the correct answer for each question.

1. _____ occurs when one food allergen comes into contact with another food item. *

   Mark only one oval.

   ◯ Cross-contamination

   ◯ Cross-contact

   ◯ Cross-connection

   ◯ Cross-inversion

2. Food allergy symptoms can show up as early as _____. *

   Mark only one oval.

   ◯ 6-8 hours

   ◯ a few minutes

   ◯ 2-3 days

   ◯ 14 days

3. Which of these is the most severe food allergy symptom? *

   Mark only one oval.

   ◯ Hives or rash

   ◯ Swelling

   ◯ Anaphylactic Shock

   ◯ Itching

136

4. Choose all of The Big 9 Allergens from the list below. (You should select 9 items   *
from the list.)

Check all that apply.

- ☐ Eggs
- ☐ Soy
- ☐ Fish
- ☐ Chocolate
- ☐ Tree Nuts
- ☐ Wheat
- ☐ Citrus Fruits
- ☐ Shellfish
- ☐ Tomatoes
- ☐ Sesame
- ☐ Milk
- ☐ Peanuts
- ☐ Kale

5. A dine-in customer asks a waitress questions about what is in the "Secret Sauce".   *
What should the waitress do?

Mark only one oval.

- ◯ Tell the customer that this information is secret for a reason and that they cannot disclose it
- ◯ Inform the customer of every ingredient in the sauce
- ◯ Tell the customer that they are not sure what is in the sauce, but let the customer know that they should be ok with ordering the sauce
- ◯ Give the customer a general idea, but not 100% factual information about what is in the sauce

6. Which statement is NOT true about Front of House staff? *

Mark only one oval.

◯ They do not have to be trained on food allergies because they do not prepare food

◯ They are the first point of contact for customers

◯ They need to know every ingredient found in all menu items

◯ They need know how to properly place special orders for guests with food allergies

Serving Food Review

Directions: Read each question below and choose the correct answer for each question.

1. Food served at sit-down restaurants, buffets, and catering events _____. *

   Mark only one oval.

   ◯ can be held at a temperature as low as 100°F as long as it is considered hot food

   ◯ can be held at a temperature as low as 100°F as long as the temperature in the room does not go over 70°F

   ◯ should be honestly presented with no food coloring or other misleading items

   ◯ can be held without temperature control for up to 8 hours

2. Bread baskets may be refilled/reused without sanitizing as long as the server is returning the item back to the same table. *

   Mark only one oval.

   ◯ True

   ◯ False

3. Cold food such as coleslaw and potato salad can be held up to _____ without temperature control as long as the temperature of the food does not go above 70°F. *

   Mark only one oval.

   ◯ 4 hours

   ◯ 8 hours

   ◯ 6 hours

   ◯ 12 hours

4. How should a server handle glasses and cups when bussing a table? *

Mark only one oval.

- By the mouthpiece
- By food-contact surfaces
- By the base or middle, or with a rack
- By whichever side is quickest and easiest for them to pickup

5. What type of food cannot be served in a restaurant that serves a group from the YOPI population or an HSP? *

Mark only one oval.

- Meat that contains a lot of fat
- Raw and undercooked foods
- Thoroughly cooked foods
- Pasteurized eggs

6. What can be served from one table to another without cleaning or sanitizing? *

Mark only one oval.

- Bread baskets
- Unwrapped eating utensils
- Unused drinkware
- Unopened and prepackaged food

7. Food should be served in equipment made from _____. *

Mark only one oval.

- ⬭ food grade materials
- ⬭ lead
- ⬭ copper
- ⬭ zinc

8. Which of these is NOT a recommendation for buffets and self-service areas? *

Mark only one oval.

- ⬭ Sneeze guards
- ⬭ Shared utensils for similarly cooked items
- ⬭ Employees monitoring the buffet area
- ⬭ Signage that informs customers that a clean plate is required for each trip to the buffet bar

9. Hot food at a catered event can be left out up to _____ hours with no temperature *
control.

Mark only one oval.

- ⬭ 2 hours
- ⬭ 4 hours
- ⬭ 6 hours
- ⬭ 8 hours

10. How should the server handle flatware when bussing a table? *

Mark only one oval.

⭕ By the mouthpiece

⭕ By food-contact surfaces

⭕ By whichever side is quickest and easiest for them to pickup

⭕ By the handle

11. Which type of animal is allowed on outdoor patios and in other dining areas as *
allowed by the establishment?

Mark only one oval.

⭕ Service dogs only

⭕ Pet dogs only

⭕ Both pet dogs and service dogs

⭕ Neither pet dogs and service dogs

12. What CANNOT be used to prepare drinks? *

Mark only one oval.

⭕ Freshly washed and sanitized utensils

⭕ Food Grade Equipment

⭕ Potable Water

⭕ Ice used to keep food cold

13. Guests are allowed to use their own take home containers in restaurants.

Mark only one oval.

⭕ True

⭕ False

YOPI Review

Directions: Read each question below and choose the correct answer for each question.

1. What does the Y in YOPI stand for? *

   Mark only one oval.

   ⬭ Young

   ⬭ Yeast

   ⬭ Yellow

   ⬭ Yield

2. What does the O in YOPI stand for? *

   Mark only one oval.

   ⬭ Omit

   ⬭ Oil

   ⬭ Old

   ⬭ Oversee

3. What does the P in YOPI stand for? *

   Mark only one oval.

   ⬭ Practice

   ⬭ Promote

   ⬭ Pregnant

   ⬭ Preview

4. What does the I in YOPI stand for? *

Mark only one oval.

○ Innocent

○ Immunocompromised

○ Indicate

○ Ice

5. Why do infants and young children have a higher risk for getting a foodborne   *
illness?

Mark only one oval.

○ They do not have strong appetites

○ They have not build up strong immune systems

○ They do not receive enough nutrition

○ They are more likely to suffer allergic reactions

Active Managerial Control Review

Directions: Read each question below and choose the correct answer for each question.

1. Active Managerial Control involves the manager or PIC _____. *

   Mark only one oval.

   ⬭ managing the food handling staff to ensure the operation is fully staffed at all times

   ⬭ controlling the amount of customers that are allowed in the operation at one time

   ⬭ managing the kitchen in order to prevent the five most common risk factors of foodborne illness

   ⬭ managing the Master Cleaning Schedule

2. The State and Local Regulatory Authority's #1 job is to protect _____. *

   Mark only one oval.

   ⬭ the restaurant owner

   ⬭ all food handlers in the operation

   ⬭ the kitchen manager

   ⬭ the general public

3. What does HACCP stand for? *

   Mark only one oval.

   ⬭ Hepatitis A Collection and Control Procedures

   ⬭ Hazard Analysis Critical Control Point

   ⬭ Healthy Adults Creating Culinary Processes

   ⬭ Hazard Application Control and Collection Protocols

4. What is the purpose of a variance? *

Mark only one oval.

- ◯ It gives the operation permission to cook items between the hours of 3am-5am
- ◯ It gives the food handler permission to wear a medical bracelet in the kitchen
- ◯ It gives the operation permission to cook food items outside of the Food Code
- ◯ It gives the food handler permission to introduce new recipes to the already established restaurant menu

5. What agency issues a variance? *

Mark only one oval.

- ◯ State and Local Regulatory Authority
- ◯ FDA
- ◯ USDA
- ◯ NSF or ANSI

6. The Health Inspector works for which agency? *

Mark only one oval.

- ◯ State and Local Regulatory Authority
- ◯ FDA
- ◯ CDC
- ◯ Mayor's Health Task Force

7. When is a variance NOT required? *

   Mark only one oval.

   ◯ When cooking chicken to a minimum internal temperature of 165°F

   ◯ When curing meat

   ◯ When using Reduce Oxygen Packaging (ROP)

   ◯ When canning or pickling

8. Which one listed below is NOT considered an imminent health hazard? *

   Mark only one oval.

   ◯ Power outage

   ◯ Authorized persons in the kitchen area

   ◯ Sewage backup

   ◯ Water Main Break

9. Who should the operation notify if there is an imminent health hazard? *

   Mark only one oval.

   ◯ FDA

   ◯ USDA

   ◯ State and Local Regulatory Authority

   ◯ CDC

10. An imminent health hazard may require the operation to be immediately shutdown.   *

    Mark only one oval.

    ◯ True

    ◯ False

11. A PIC must be on-site at all times at which of the following:

Mark only one oval.

- ◯ Market without cashiers
- ◯ Privately owned 24-hour pancake diner
- ◯ Convenience store
- ◯ All of these require a PIC on-site at all times
- ◯ None of these require a PIC on-site at all times

12. Who gives an establishment permission to continue service after the establishment has corrected problems associated with an imminent health hazard? *

Mark only one oval.

- ◯ FDA
- ◯ State and Local Regulatory Authority
- ◯ USDA
- ◯ CDC

ANSWER KEY

ANSWER KEY FOR REVIEW QUESTIONS

Food Safety Temperature Review
1. 70°F to 125°F
2. 135°F
3. 41°F
4. 41°F
5. 4
6. 2:30 pm
7. 135°F
8. 41°F to 135°F
9. Every 2 hours
10. Reject the carton

Temperature/Time Controlled for Safety Review
1. Uncooked garbanzo beans
2. 7 days
3. Sprouts
4. Ceviche
5. Food, Acidity, Temperature, Time, Oxygen, Moisture
6. Cooked Brown Rice
7. Lemon/lime juice
8. Olive oil infused with garlic and herbs
9. Raw ground turkey or raw ground beef
10. Coffee

Types of Contamination Review
1. Informs staff of safe use and hazards of chemical used in the operation
2. False
3. Handwashing
4. Bacteria
5. Hair and Hair accessories
6. Intentional/Deliberate
7. Assure
8. Look
9. Employees
10. Reports
11. Threat

Cleaning & Sanitizing Review
1. Every 4 hours
2. Every 24 hours
3. Food Contact Surfaces
4. Master Cleaning Schedule

5. Wash, rinse, and sanitize the three-compartment sink
6. Scrape or remove food, wash, rinse, sanitize, air-dry
7. Sanitize
8. All of these are approved chemicals for sanitizing
9. At least 110°F
10. Use test strips to measure the concentration of chemical in the water

Cleaning & Sanitizing Review (2)
1. Iodine and Quats
2. Chlorine/Bleach
3. parts per million
4. 50-99 ppm
5. 12.5-25 ppm
6. Differs based on Manufacture Recommendations
7. Water Color
8. All of these statements are true about cleaning products.
9. True
10. 110°F
11. 180°F
12. False
13. Detergent and hot water, clean water, sanitizer

Cleaning & Sanitizing Review (3)
1. Service Sink
2. In a dirty linen bag
3. Below work tables and at least 6 inches off the floor
4. Every 4 hours
5. Hanging on a hook

Purchasing & Receiving Food Review
1. Approved and Reputable
2. Air probe
3. Key drop delivery
4. Surface probe
5. Immediately
6. 2
7. Cold/ice water calibration
8. Before and after each use
9. Immersion probe
10. Penetration probe
11. Time-Temperature Indicator (TTI)

Purchasing & Receiving Food Review (2)

1. Must be commercially raised for food
2. Store food items in the refrigerator
3. Food was held, prepared and packaged according to the Food Code
4. In the warmest part of the cooler
5. 45°F
6. 90 days from the day the last item has been sold or served from the bag
7. In the coolest part of the oven
8. 90 days
9. To help control parasites
10. Must come from approved foragers to control toxins
11. In the warmest part of a walk-in storage cooler

Minimum Internal Cooking Temperature Review

1. To warn customers about the risks of eating raw and undercooked foods
2. Cook them items according to the instructions on the package
3. 165°F
4. 135°F held for a minimum of 15 seconds
5. 145°F held for a minimum of 15 seconds
6. 145°F held for a minimum of 15 seconds
7. 155°F held for a minimum of 17 seconds
8. 155°F
9. 155°F
10. 165°F
11. 145°F
12. 155°F
13. 60
14. 41°F
15. True
16. Cooked to the correct minimum internal cooking temperature

Cooling Food Review

1. 2 hours
2. 4 hours
3. 6 hours
4. A cooldown log
5. Larger portions
6. Food must be cooled to 34°F within 7 days of reaching 41°F

Facility Requirements Review

1. Reduce sharpness between the floor and wall and make the floor easier to sweep
2. Smooth, durable, and easy to clean
3. Have a protective shield or protective lens
4. Hoods and proper ventilation system

5. Cross-connection
6. Water flows in reverse due to a change in pressure within the plumbing system
7. Air gap
8. They allow water to flow in one direction
9. Prepared & Unprepared
10. Vacuum breaker
11. NSF, ANSI, or ANAB
12. CDC Certification mark

Facility Requirements Review (2)
1. 6 inches
2. 4 inches
3. Casters/wheels
4. Be leakproof, waterproof, and easy to clean
5. Have tight fitting lids and be sitting on concrete/asphalt
6. Shelter
7. Installing an air gap
8. Licensed Pest Control Operator
9. Be mounted to the floor
10. All of these are things that you should deny pests

SHENS Review
1. Hepatitis A
2. Salmonella
3. Norovirus
4. E. Coli
5. Shigella
6. Hepatitis A
7. Regular and Typhi/Typhoid
8. Liver
9. They have been symptom-free for at least 24 hours and they have been cleared by a note from their doctor
10. Jaundice

SHENS Review (2)
1. Can work in the operation, but they cannot work around food
2. Cannot come to work at all
3. Jaundice
4. Sore throat
5. Must be excluded from the operation until cleared by a note from their doctor
6. Should not come to work at all
7. Feces
8. Vomiting and Diarrhea
9. Employee Health Policy Agreement

10. State and Local Regulatory Authority

FAT TOM Review
1. 41°F to 135°F
2. Food
3. Acidity
4. Temperature and Time
5. Oxygen
6. Moisture
7. With a low pH value (neutral to slightly acidic)
8. High
9. 70°F to 125°F
10. The opportunity for bacteria to grow to unsafe levels increases

Foodborne Illness Review
1. Issues the Food Code
2. Inspects meat, poultry, and eggs packaging
3. CDC
4. Foodborne illness
5. Outbreak
6. Unsafe
7. False
8. Cook
9. Incorrect
10. Contaminated
11. Poor
12. It occurs when food is cooked to the right temperature, but it is cooked too long

Personal Hygiene Review
1. Hot & Cold Water, Soap, Single Use Paper Towel (or way to dry hands), Garbage Container, Signage
2. 20 seconds
3. 10-15 seconds
4. 85°F
5. Carrier
6. FDA
7. 60%
8. Band-Aid and Glove/Finger Cot
9. Smooth plain band ring
10. Wash your hands
11. Only after washing your hands

Personal Hygiene Review (2)

1. True
2. When washing produce or when handling foods that will be properly cooked
3. 1/4 inch
4. Clean apron and hat/hair net
5. Take off their aprons
6. Should have a lid and a straw, a label with their name on it, and be stored away from food prep areas
7. Outside and away from food prep areas
8. False
9. Nail polish
10. Because most pizza ovens reach a temperature of at least 450°F and pathogens will be killed at this temperature
11. Smoking outside the building at the food service establishment
12. False eyelashes
13. Wash their hands
14. Waterproof/impermeable dressing that is durable and tight-fitting, and a glove

Preparing Food Review

1. White
2. Cross-contamination
3. Wash, rinse, and sanitize equipment
4. In the order that the items go in the refrigerator
5. Blue
6. Red
7. Green
8. Brown
9. Purple

Preparing and Storing Food Review

1. Pasteurized Eggs
2. 70°F
3. On the countertop
4. Have a label with a common name
5. 7 days
6. 24 hours
7. Have a label with a common name and a discard date
8. Be packaged with a label that shows the ingredients in descending order by weight
9. Items with earliest use-by/discard dates are stored in front of items with later use-by/discard dates
10. Date Made + 6 days

Food Allergies Review
1. Cross-contact
2. A few minutes
3. Anaphylactic Shock
4. Eggs, Soy, Fish, Tree Nuts, Wheat, Shellfish, Sesame, Milk, Peanuts
5. Inform the customer of every ingredient in the "Secret Sauce"
6. They do not have to be trained on food allergies because they do not prepare food

Serving Food Review
1. Should be honestly presented with no food coloring or other misleading items
2. True
3. 6 hours
4. By the base or middle, or with a rack
5. Raw and undercooked foods
6. Unopened and prepackaged food
7. Food grade materials
8. Shared utensils for similarly cooked items
9. 4 hours
10. By the handle
11. Both pet dogs and service dogs
12. Ice used to keep food cold
13. False

YOPI Review
1. Young
2. Old
3. Pregnant
4. Immunocompromised
5. They have not build up strong immune systems

Active Managerial Control Review
1. Managing the kitchen in order to prevent the five most common risk factors of foodborne illness
2. The general public
3. Hazard Analysis Critical Control Point
4. It gives the operation permission to cook food items outside of the Food Code
5. State and Local Regulatory Authority
6. State and Local Regulatory Authority
7. When cooking chicken to a minimum internal temperature of 165°F
8. Authorized persons in the kitchen area
9. State and Local Regulatory Authority
10. True
11. Privately owned 24-hour pancake diner
12. State and Local Regulatory Authority

Made in the USA
Columbia, SC
23 July 2024